Human Rights

Edited by
A. I. Melden
University of California, Irvine

Wadsworth Publishing Company, Inc.   Belmont, California

To Rob

L. C. Cat. Card No.: 76–126769
Printed in the United States of America

7 8 9 10 — 80 79

Contents

Introduction 1

The Second Treatise of Civil Government, Chapters 2 and 5
John Locke 10

Anarchical Fallacies
Jeremy Bentham 28

Natural Rights
Margaret MacDonald 40

Are There Any Natural Rights?
H. L. A. Hart 61

Justice and Equality
Gregory Vlastos 76

Rights, Human Rights, and Racial Discrimination
Richard Wasserstrom 96

Persons and Punishment
Herbert Morris 111

Appendices
  I. The Virginia Declaration of Rights, June 12, 1776 135

II. Extract from the Declaration of Independence of the United States of America, July 4, 1776   138

III. Declaration of the Rights of Man and of Citizens (1789)   140

IV. Universal Declaration of Human Rights   143

Bibliography   150

Series Foreword

The Basic Problems in Philosophy Series is designed to meet the need of students and teachers of philosophy, mainly but not exclusively at the undergraduate level, for collections of essays devoted to some fairly specific philosophical problems.

In recent years there have been numerous paperback collections on a variety of philosophical topics. Those teachers who wish to refer their students to a set of essays on a specific philosophical problem have usually been frustrated, however, since most of these collections range over a wide set of issues and problems. The present series attempts to remedy this situation by presenting together, within each volume, key writings on a single philosophical issue.

Given the magnitude of the literature, there can be no thought of completeness. Rather, the materials included are those that, in the judgment of the editor, must be mastered first by the student who wishes to acquaint himself with relevant issues and their ramifications. To this end, historical as well as contemporary writings will be included.

Each volume in the series will contain an introduction by the editor to set the stage for the arguments contained in the essays and a bibliography to help the student who wishes to pursue the topic at a more advanced level.

A. I. Melden
S. Munsat

Basic Problems in Philosophy Series

A. I. Melden and Stanley Munsat
University of California, Irvine
General Editors

Human Rights
A. I. Melden

Introduction   The Second Treatise of Civil Government, Chapters 2 and 5. *John Locke*   Anarchical Fallacies. *Jeremy Bentham*   Natural Rights. *Margaret MacDonald*   Are There Any Natural Rights? *H. L. A. Hart*   Justice and Equality. *Gregory Vlastos*   Rights, Human Rights, and Racial Discrimination. *Richard Wasserstrom*   Persons and Punishment. *Herbert Morris*   Appendices   Bibliography

Guilt and Shame
Herbert Morris

Introduction   Stavrogin's Confession. *Fyodor Dostoyevsky*   Differentiation of German Guilt. *Karl Jaspers*   Origin of the Sense of Guilt. *Sigmund Freud*   Guilt and Guilt Feelings. *Martin Buber*   Real Guilt and Neurotic Guilt. *Herbert Fingarette*   "Guilt," "Bad Conscience," and the Like. *Friedrich Nietzsche*   The Sense of Justice. *John Rawls*   Shame. *Gerhart Piers and Milton B. Singer*   Autonomy v. Shame and Doubt. *Erik H. Erikson*   The Nature of Shame. *Helen Merrell Lynd*   Bibliography

The Analytic-Synthetic Distinction
Stanley Munsat

Introduction   First Truths. *Gottfried Wilhelm von Leibniz*   Necessary and Contingent Truths. *Gottfried Wilhelm von Leibniz*   Of Proposition. *Thomas Hobbes*   Introduction to the Critique of Pure Reason. *Immanuel Kant*   Kant. *Arthur Papp*   Of Demonstration, and Necessary Truths. *John Stuart Mill*   Views of Some Writers on the Nature of Arithmetical Propositions. *Gottlob Frege*   What Is an Empirical Science? *Bertrand Russell*   Two Dogmas of Empiricism. *Willard Van Orman Quine*   The Meaning of a Word. *John Austin*   In Defense of a Dogma. *H. P. Grice and P. F. Strawson*   Bibliography

Civil Disobedience and Violence
Jeffrie G. Murphy

Introduction   On Disobeying the Law. *Socrates*   On the Duty of Civil Disobedience. *Henry David Thoreau*   Legal Obligation and the Duty of Fair Play. *John Rawls*   Social Protest and Civil Obedience. *Sydney Hook*   The Vietnam War and the Right of Resistance. *Jeffrie G. Murphy*   Civil Disobedience: Prerequisite for Democracy in Mass Society. *Christian Bay*   Non-violence. *Mohandas K. Gandhi*   A Fallacy on Law and Order: That Civil Disobedience Must Be Absolutely Nonviolent. *Howard Zinn*   On Not Prosecuting Civil Disobedience. *Ronald Dworkin*   Law and Authority. *Peter Kropotkin*   Bibliography

Morality and the Law
Richard A. Wasserstrom

Introduction   On Liberty, *John Stuart Mill*   Morals and the Criminal Law, *Lord Patrick Devlin*   Immorality and Treason, *H. L. A. Hart* Lord Devlin and the Enforcement of Morals, *Ronald Dworkin*   Sins and Crimes, *A. R. Louch*   Morals Offenses and the Model Penal Code, *Louis B. Schwartz*   Paternalism, *Gerald Dworkin*   Four cases involving the enforcement of morality   Bibliography

War and Morality
Richard A. Wasserstrom

Introduction   The Moral Equivalent of War, *William James*   The Morality of Obliteration Bombing, *John C. Ford, S.J.*   War and Murder, *Elizabeth Anscombe*   Moral Judgment in Time of War, *Michael Walzer* Pacifism: A Philosophical Analysis, *Jan Narveson*   On the Morality of War: A Preliminary Inquiry, *Richard Wasserstrom*   Judgment and Opinion, The International Tribunal, Nuremberg, Germany   Superior Orders, Nuclear Warfare, and the Dictates of Conscience, *Guenter Lewy* Selected Bibliography

Introduction

Moral rights are based on many different sorts of circumstance. Some are acquired by virtue of some act or performance. For example, a promise made to someone gives the latter a right, the correlative of which is the obligation assumed by the promiser. Some moral rights are acquired by assuming some office, as in the case of someone who undertakes to serve as chairman of some organization. Some are connected with a relation in which one stands to others within a family group, as in the case of a father with respect to his son. In each of these cases the question "What gives him the right to . . . ?," occasioned by what may appear to be unusual privilege, can be answered by reference to that which, very broadly, can be described as a social fact or circumstance.

According to many, however, there can be another and quite different response to this sort of question when posed by the perhaps insensitive or superficial observer, namely, "He is, after all, a human being." Such a reply implies that independently of the specific and variable social facts about human beings, indeed (as Vlastos notes in the essay included in this volume) independently of the merit that human beings may achieve, there is good and sufficient reason for ascribing rights to them, namely, the mere fact that they are human beings.

Such a view has its origin in doctrines held long ago. The Stoics maintained that there is a natural law, distinct from the laws of Athens or Rome, a law binding upon all men in such a manner that "whoever is disobedient is fleeing from himself and denying his human nature."[1] Some have traced the doctrine all the way back to Plato and Aristotle in their denial of moral conventionalism (the view that morality is simply a matter of convention); for both attempted, albeit in different ways, to give an account of morality in terms of the nature of man. Certainly the seventeenth century conception of natural rights

[1] Cicero, *The Republic*, Book 3.

adumbrated by Locke had its more immediate antecedent in
the medieval conception of a Natural Law instilled in man's
mind by God himself: a Law discoverable not by the Stoic test
of universal assent, but rather by reason as well as by examination of Holy Scripture; a Law that is no mere common
denominator, as it were, of the laws of Athens and Rome, but
the commandment of God; and a Law that serves as the test,
not merely of the justice of the positive laws of particular
states, but of their very force as law itself.[2] There are, however,
differences between the Lockean doctrine of natural rights and
the earlier tradition of natural law. This Lockean doctrine
introduced new features which were important to men of practical affairs who put them to use in the political upheavals that
took place not only in England but also in America and in
France. For the natural rights movement that developed in the
seventeenth century, and of which John Locke was the notable
exponent, emphasized (as H. L. A. Hart observes in the essay
included in this volume) something one finds missing in medieval statements of natural law, namely, the idea that there are
rights that persons have in addition to the fact that there are
right acts that may be demanded of them.

For the notion of a right that is one's moral title opens up a
complex conceptual structure in which the notion of a right is
embedded, a structure that is of considerable importance for
the implications it carries for the conception of a moral agent.
For, given this notion of a moral right, we must now think of
persons not only as beings doing or failing to do what is
required of them, but as beings who in their dealings with one
another may claim, assert, demand, exercise, or waive, relin-
quish, transfer, or perhaps even forfeit the rights that they
have. And in the event that their rights are violated they may
claim for themselves, and not merely through the intercession
of sympathetic persons acting on their behalf, the redress that
is due them. Such claims are made by those who are capable
of self-respect and moral dignity. They are not appeals to the
benevolence or largesse of those who have done them injury,
to desist from burdening them with unkindness or unpleasantness. They are, rather, claims made by free agents calling for
redress for the *moral* damage they have suffered. Indeed, if
there are moral rights that agents can thus demand and assert,

---

[2] See Aquinas, who quotes with approval the dictum of Augustine that
that which is not just seems to be no law at all. *Treatise on Law,* from the
First Part of the *Summa Theologica,* Question 91, Article 4, in the edition
by A. C. Pegis published by Random House, New York, 1945, Vol. 2, pp.
794–796.

then it is at least plausible to argue, as Hart and others have, that there must be some right or rights that are fundamental to them, namely, a right or set of rights that may be called human or natural. For this is part and parcel of what has been intended by the advocates of the traditional doctrine of natural rights and more recently, by those who have argued that there are human rights: (1) that these rights are fundamental in the sense that without them there could not be any of the specific rights that are grounded in the specific social circumstances in which individuals live, (2) that just as these rights cannot be acquired by anything they or others may do, so they cannot be relinquished, transferred, or forfeited (i.e., they cannot be alienated from them by anything that they or anyone else may do), since (3) they are rights that human beings have simply because they are human beings, and quite independently of their varying social circumstances and degrees of merit.

If this is granted, the lesson can be drawn, as it was by Locke and his followers, that there are limits to the power that governments may rightly wield, and sufficient grounds for extraordinary political action when the inalienable rights of persons are violated. For the violation of these fundamental rights by tyrants, governments, or any others becomes the violation of the very humanity of individuals—the threatened or actual destruction of their status and the dignity they have as human beings. Such a destruction of a person, which is no mere taking of the life of another, involves a degradation and a demeaning of human life that evokes the most profound revulsion. And the call to action in order to combat such evil is, as Macdonald observed, far more inspiring than the complaint that there is need to promote the pleasures or to improve the happiness or well-being of our fellows by changing the institutions under which they live. It is only when natural or human rights are so understood that it is intelligible to us, as it was to the political activists of the seventeenth and eighteenth centuries, that a violation of the rights of man provides sufficient incentive for heroism and even self-sacrifice.

Of particular interest to Locke's followers was his list of the natural rights of men. These consisted not only of the rights that men have to their lives and to the liberty to order them in accordance with their aspirations, but also to property, which he thought they may acquire independently of any legislation, judicial decision, or social institution. No doubt the claim that there is a natural right to property was particularly appealing to the rising middle class of the time. But there are confusions, ambiguities, and fatal difficulties in Locke's discussion of the right. For given the severing of any conceptual tie between property and legal statutes, a severing which Bentham among others rejected as absurd, the concept of property becomes nebulous indeed. For it is now applied by Locke to that which is made part of oneself, as in the case of food when eaten,[3] and even to one's own person[4] on what appears to be the tenuous verbal ground that the fact that the food that a man has taken into his mouth, like the person of a man, provides us with something in common with the watch he owns, namely, that all of these varied items can be said to be his. But, basically, Locke presents us with a labor theory of property by which he attempts to explain how it is that, quite independently of legislation, judicial decision, or the consent of anyone else, the "turf my servant has cut, and the ore I have digged in any place, where I have a right to them in common with others (this being the case with all things in the state of nature), become my property," namely, by virtue of the labor expended.[5] The difficulties posed by this view are legion, as later writers were quick to observe, not the least of which is the enormous difference between the case of some Robinson Crusoe making a flute from a branch cut from a tree in a forest on some unknown island by means of implements which he himself produced (here recognizably he makes the flute *his* merely by the labor he expends) and the labor expended in the making of an article in the circumstances of a complex society, where it would be difficult indeed to draw the line between those who have not and those who have, even in the most oblique and indirect ways, made their contribution to the production of some article. There is irony too in the Marxist's familiar denunciation of the exploitation of workers, in that this suggests that very labor theory of property that was advanced in the seventeenth century by Locke, the great spokesman for the rising middle class. But there is also injustice in the criticism of Locke by the Marxist that he was concerned simply with property rights and saw the state merely as a means to their protection. The source of this criticism is Locke's view, repeated in a number of places, that "the great and chief end . . . of men's uniting into commonwealths and putting themselves under government, is the preservation of their property."[6] But this is to ignore the explanation given in the immedi-

---

[3] Cf. the second of Locke's *Two Treatises of Civil Government,* Chap. 5, paragraph 26.

[4] *Ibid.,* paragraph 27.

[5] *Ibid.,* paragraph 28.

[6] *Ibid.,* Chap. 9, paragraph 124.

ately preceding sentence—and repeated elsewhere—that the term "property" is to be used to cover not only men's estates but their lives and their liberties.

For most writers on the topic, however, the objections to the doctrine of natural rights which Bentham raised have seemed insurmountable. Directing his attack against the French Assembly's Declaration of the Rights of Man (but intending it, presumably, to apply to earlier American Declarations and to the views of Locke himself), Bentham takes the doctrine of natural, imprescriptible rights to life, liberty, and property to be the doctrine that these are unbounded rights, that in respect of each of them a man may do as he pleases, rejecting all social restraints including the risks to life and limb incurred when a state requires the military services of its citizens, all taxes and all penalties of punishment including capital punishment itself. No doubt the call "to let freedom ring" that one hears these days from some on the extreme political right is intended to serve as the rallying cry for those committed to the absolute right to property, where "absolute right" means a right one may exercise as one pleases. Against such utterances, Bentham argued effectively enough; and his description of them as rhetorical and mischievous nonsense, nonsense upon stilts, seems justified. But whatever may have been intended by the authors of the French Assembly's Declaration, this is most surely not the view of Locke. For in his discussion of the power that a prince or senate may rightly exercise (i.e., their right, which in his view is derived from the consent of the governed), Locke goes on to discuss the absolute power that a military commander may, in Locke's opinion, exercise in order to show that, *even here,* the power may not be exercised arbitrarily. Clearly what is at issue here is the absolute right that, in Locke's opinion, an officer has vis à vis the soldiers under his command. And here, quite explicitly, he tells us that even in this case "absolute power, when it is necessary, is not arbitrary by being absolute, but is still limited by that reason, and confined to those ends which required it."[7] Clearly a right that is absolute is *not* a right that may be exercised as one pleases. Nor is an absolute right one which requires no circumstances, no basis in fact, for the person or body that has it. A military commander, so Locke thought, has the absolute right to order his troops to march up to the mouths of cannon, and thus to face death; but this right is one that he has by virtue of his function as commander of a military organization whose end is

---

[7] *Ibid.,* Chap. 9, paragraph 139.

the defense of his country and the protection of the lives of citizens. And a human being has his absolute rights by virtue of that nature with which God endowed him. Beyond these facts nothing *further,* as Locke saw it, is required for the absolute rights that military commanders and human beings have. Such absolute rights contrast with conditional rights, e.g., the right of a military commander to withhold for later payment part of a soldier's pay, a right which a commander has only on the condition that an agreement to that effect has been properly executed, and the right of a man to vote, which is conditional upon his satisfying a number of conditions specified by statutes. An absolute right does not confer capricious or unreasonable powers; neither a conditional nor an absolute right is a right to do what one pleases or what suits one's passing fancy. Even an absolute right "is limited by that reason, and confined to those ends which required it."

The text of the *Second Treatise* also demonstrates that Locke was well aware of the fact that punishment may deprive a man of his property, his liberty, and even his life. For many, from Bentham on down to contemporary philosophers, this has been either ignored or attributed to gross inconsistency and, like other difficulties in Locke's discussion, has been regarded as one more nail in the coffin to which the doctrine of natural rights must be consigned.

But does a man lose a right if, justifiably, he is prevented from exercising it? Locke does not explicitly distinguish, as others have done in more recent days, between having a right and being justified in exercising, asserting, or claiming it.[8] But it is not at all far fetched to suggest that a distinction such as this is implied by him given his stipulation that even in the case of a right that confers absolute power, that power "is limited by that reason, and confined to those ends which required it." Does a man, then, forfeit his right to life when, as Locke himself concedes, justice may require that he lose his life on the gallows? To the suggestion that he forfeits his life, not his right to life, it will be retorted that it is an empty right indeed when in such cases there is no possible exercise of that right, since the man himself is dead. Certainly a man's death cannot be undone; a man's life is not like some item of property or liberty, something that he can lose but then on a subsequent occasion have restored to him. But forfeiting one's life in such a case as this is not synonymous with losing one's status as a human being—that can happen through degeneration. Losing

[8] Cf. my *Rights and Right Conduct,* Oxford, 1959, pp. 18 ff.

one's life on the gallows is not to be identified with being destroyed as a person; for the latter can happen without his life's being taken. In any case, even on the gallows the man is treated as a man, not as an ant whose life may be rubbed out at will. What is required even here, and this is what Locke insists upon even in the case of those absolute powers over others that are conferred by rights, is that the power must not be exercised capriciously or arbitrarily, but "is limited by that reason . . . that required it." And this is to say that the right in question that confers such extreme power is no automatic license to its exercise on any occasion that suits or pleases one, but may be exercised only under the limits imposed by reason. Thus, there may indeed be more consistency and good sense in Locke on this point than many of his eager critics have imagined, and have exhibited in the course of their argument that justified capital punishment is inconsistent with the supposition that there is a natural right to life.[9]

There are, however, real difficulties in Locke's account. Because of these and the reluctance of most philosophers to accept the theological doctrine that served as an important support for Locke's theory of natural rights, most thinkers until relatively recent times have relegated the doctrine of natural or human rights to a curious chapter of the dead past, the echoes of which, however, can be detected in the political rhetoric employed on ceremonial occasions.

But the horrors of Nazi Germany, of such a degree and on such a vast scale that post-World War II generations can scarcely apprehend, were enough to shock not only the conscience of mankind, but also the complacency with which the earlier doctrine of natural rights had been summarily dismissed.[10] And the brutalities perpetrated upon black minorities in South Africa, together with the growing recognition in America that many forms of segregation of such minorities in America amount, as Wasserstrom reminds us, to "reading certain persons . . . out of the human race,"[11] have helped to revive philosophical interest in the concept of universal human rights.

Perhaps the earliest attempt by a professional philosopher in the post-World War II period to pay heed to the insight, how-

---

[9] It is of some interest to note in this connection the contention that "due process" of law is *the* constitutional protection of the right to life. Cf. H. Bedau, "The Right to Life," *The Monist*, Vol. 52, No. 4 (October 1968), p. 562.

[10] See *The Universal Declaration of Human Rights*, adopted in 1948 by the General Assembly of the United Nations, in Appendix IV.

[11] See his essay in this volume.

ever distorted and confused it might be, which was contained in the older doctrine of natural rights, is the essay by Margaret Macdonald which first appeared in 1947. In some respects, this essay is a period piece. The concern here is with the nature of the "value judgment" that persons have natural rights, and with the factual basis for such declarations. Repudiating any attempt to identify such "values" with any "natural fact" and rejecting the intuitionist's search for values in some supersensible realm, Macdonald is led to assimilate the ascription to men of natural rights, not to a proposition about such rights, but to something else, namely, the announcement of the decision, "This is where I stand." But later writers, on the whole, have not subscribed to the constricting epistemology that underlies her discussion, and that narrows the range of fact to what is "empirically verifiable," in that rather special way that led empiricists of the 1940s to ethical emotivism. And well they might be free of this sort of preconception. For while Margaret Macdonald does insist that saying that a human being has natural rights is no mere substitute for a smile or a tear, the saying, she thinks, consists in the announcement of a decision. And given the narrow view she takes of "fact," in consequence of which "human being" is construed in a wholly non-normative way, the decision surely stands in need of justification. But what is left of the very notion of decision itself, for which, in principle, no justification in terms of any matters of fact would appear possible, is difficult indeed to make out. For if there are facts about human beings such that they do justify the ascription to them of human rights, then it would appear to follow from those matters of human fact that there are such human rights. But if this is so, then the concept of a human being cannot be so far divorced from our moral notions that it is, as the empiricists of the time took it to be, wholly devoid of any normative import.

More recently, there are important respects in which progress has been made. To begin with, the essays by Hart, Vlastos, Wasserstrom, and Morris all deal sympathetically, though in different ways, with the concept of human rights, and this is indeed characteristic of the treatment of this concept in philosophical circles since World War II. For even among those who do think that a man forfeits not only his life but his right to life when he receives the capital punishment due him, there are philosophers who concede that human beings *qua* human beings do have the right to life, but declare that this human right is only a *prima facie* right, where, whatever they do mean by a *prima facie* right, they certainly do *not* mean a right that is merely apparent or presumptive.[12] As these essays also show, there has been an increased understanding of the very notion of a right as an entitlement, a far greater appreciation of the complexity of the conceptual framework in which this notion has its place in our moral thinking, together with a better sense of the fact that an appeal to a right provides a justification for conduct. And, finally, in dealing sympathetically with our everyday talk about the rights that human beings have, these essays exhibit a much clearer appreciation of matters of human fact, without which our philosophical thinking about morality fails to come to grips with its subject matter and dooms us to the idle talk of Milton's fallen angels, who discoursed and reasoned high "and found no end, in wandering mazes lost."

---

[12] Cf. the essay by Vlastos for a discussion of this notion of a *prima facie* right.

John Locke

The Second Treatise of Civil Government

Chapter II
Of the State of Nature

10   4. To understand political power aright, and derive it from its original, we must consider what state all men are naturally in, and that is a state of perfect freedom to order their actions and dispose of their possessions and persons as they think fit, within the bounds of the law of nature, without asking leave, or depending upon the will of any other man.

A state also of equality, wherein all the power and jurisdiction is reciprocal, no one having more than another; there being nothing more evident than that creatures of the same species and rank, promiscuously born to all the same advantages of nature, and the use of the same faculties, should also be equal one amongst another without subordination or subjection, unless the Lord and Master of them all should by any manifest declaration of His will set one above another, and confer on him by an evident and clear appointment an undoubted right to dominion and sovereignty.

5. This equality of men by nature the judicious Hooker looks upon as so evident in itself and beyond all question, that he makes it the foundation of that obligation to mutual love amongst men on which he builds the duties they owe one another, and from whence he derives the great maxims of justice and charity. His words are:—

The like natural inducement hath brought men to know that it is no less their duty to love others than themselves; for seeing those things which are equal must needs all have one measure,

Published first in 1690, the political theories contained in the *Two Treatises* by John Locke (1632–1704) played an important role in the development of parliamentary government in England. In America their influence is manifest in *The Virginian Declaration of Rights* (1776) and later in the same year in *The Declaration of Independence* (see Appendixes I and II).

if I cannot but wish to receive good, even as much at every man's hands as any man can wish unto his own soul, how should I look to have any part of my desire herein satisfied, unless myself be careful to satisfy the like desire, which is undoubtedly in other men weak, being of one and the same nature? To have anything offered them repugnant to this desire, must needs in all respects grieve them as much as me, so that, if I do harm, I must look to suffer, there being no reason that others should show greater measures of love to me than they have by me showed unto them. My desire, therefore, to be loved of my equals in nature as much as possible may be, imposeth upon me a natural duty of bearing to themward fully the like affection; from which relation of equality between ourselves and them that are as ourselves, what several rules and canons natural reason hath drawn for direction of life no man is ignorant (Eccl. Pol., lib. i).

6. But though this be a state of liberty, yet it is not a state of license; though man in that state have an uncontrollable liberty to dispose of his person or possessions, yet he has not liberty to destroy himself, or so much as any creature in his possession, but where some nobler use than its bare preservation calls for it. The state of nature has a law of nature to govern it, which obliges everyone; and reason, which is that law, teaches all mankind who will but consult it, that, being all equal and independent, no one ought to harm another in his life, health, liberty, or possessions. For men being all the workmanship of one omnipotent and infinitely wise Maker—all the servants of one sovereign Master, sent into the world by His order, and about His business—they are His property, whose workmanship they are, made to last during His, not one another's pleasure; and being furnished with like faculties, sharing all in one community of nature, there cannot be supposed any such subordination among us, that may authorize us to destroy one another, as if we were made for one another's uses, as the inferior ranks of creatures are for ours. Everyone, as he is bound to preserve himself, and not to quit his station willfully, so, by the like reason, when his own preservation comes not in competition, ought he, as much as he can, to preserve the rest of mankind, and not, unless it be to do justice on an offender, take away or impair the life, or what tends to the preservation of the life, the liberty, health, limb, or goods of another.

7. And that all men may be restrained from invading others' rights, and from doing hurt to one another, and the law of nature be observed, which willeth the peace and preservation

of all mankind, the execution of the law of nature is in that state put into every man's hand, whereby everyone has a right to punish the transgressors of that law to such a degree as may hinder its violation. For the law of nature would, as all other laws that concern men in this world, be in vain if there were nobody that, in the state of nature, had a power to execute that law, and thereby preserve the innocent and restrain offenders. And if anyone in the state of nature may punish another for any evil he has done, everyone may do so. For in that state of perfect equality, where naturally there is no superiority or jurisdiction of one over another, what any may do in prosecution of that law, everyone must needs have a right to do.

8. And thus in the state of nature one man comes by a power over another; but yet no absolute or arbitrary power, to use a criminal, when he has got him in his hands, according to the passionate heats or boundless extravagance of his own will; but only to retribute to him so far as calm reason and conscience dictate what is proportionate to his transgression, which is so much as may serve for reparation and restraint. For these two are the only reasons why one man may lawfully do harm to another, which is that we call punishment. In transgressing the law of nature, the offender declares himself to live by another rule than that of common reason and equity, which is that measure God has set to the actions of men, for their mutual security; and so he becomes dangerous to mankind, the tie which is to secure them from injury and violence being slighted and broken by him. Which, being a trespass against the whole species, and the peace and safety of it, provided for by the law of nature, every man upon this score, by the right he hath to preserve mankind in general, may restrain, or, where it is necessary, destroy things noxious to them, and so may bring such evil on anyone who hath transgressed that law, as may make him repent the doing of it, and thereby deter him, and by his example others, from doing the like mischief. And in this case, and upon this ground, every man hath a right to punish the offender, and be executioner of the law of nature.

9. I doubt not but this will seem a very strange doctrine to some men: but before they condemn it, I desire them to resolve me by what right any prince or state can put to death or punish an alien, for any crime he commits in their country. 'Tis certain their laws, by virtue of any sanction they receive from the promulgated will of the legislative, reach not a stranger: they speak not to him, nor, if they did, is he bound to hearken to them. The legislative authority, by which they are in force over

the subjects of that commonwealth, hath no power over him. Those who have the supreme power of making laws in England, France, or Holland, are to an Indian but like the rest of the world—men without authority. And, therefore, if by the law of nature every man hath not a power to punish offenses against it, as he soberly judges the case to require, I see not how the magistrates of any community can punish an alien of another country; since in reference to him they can have no more power than what every man naturally may have over another.

10. Besides the crime which consists in violating the law, and varying from the right rule of reason, whereby a man so far becomes degenerate, and declares himself to quit the principles of human nature, and to be a noxious creature, there is commonly injury done, and some person or other, some other man receives damage by his transgression, in which case he who hath received any damage, has, besides the right of punishment common to him with other men, a particular right to seek reparation from him that has done it. And any other person who finds it just, may also join with him that is injured, and assist him in recovering from the offender so much as many make satisfaction for the harm he has suffered.

11. From these two distinct rights—the one of punishing the crime for restraint and preventing the like offense, which right of punishing is in everybody; the other of taking reparation, which belongs only to the injured party—comes it to pass that the magistrate, who by being magistrate hath the common right of punishing put into his hands, can often, where the public good demands not the execution of the law, remit the punishment of criminal offenses by his own authority, but yet cannot remit the satisfaction due to any private man for the damage he has received. That he who has suffered the damage has a right to demand in his own name, and he alone can remit. The damnified person has this power of appropriating to himself the goods or service of the offender, by right of self-preservation, as every man has a power to punish the crime, to prevent its being committed again, by the right he has of preserving all mankind, and doing all reasonable things he can in order to that end. And thus it is that every man in the state of nature has a power to kill a murderer, both to deter others from doing the like injury, which no reparation can compensate, by the example of the punishment that attends it from everybody, and also to secure men from the attempts of a criminal who having renounced reason, the common rule and measure God hath given to mankind, hath by the unjust violence and slaughter he

hath committed upon one, declared war against all mankind, and therefore may be destroyed as a lion or a tiger, one of those wild savage beasts with whom men can have no society nor security. And upon this is grounded that great law of nature. "Whoso sheddeth man's blood, by man shall his blood be shed." And Cain was so fully convinced that everyone had a right to destroy such a criminal, that after the murder of his brother he cries out, "Every one that findeth me shall slay me;" so plain was it writ in the hearts of mankind.

12. By the same reason may a man in the state of nature punish the lesser breaches of that law. It will perhaps be demanded, With death? I answer, each transgression may be punished to that degree, and with so much severity, as will suffice to make it an ill bargain to the offender, give him cause to repent, and terrify others from doing the like. Every offense that can be committed in the state of nature, may in the state of nature be also punished equally, and as far forth as it may, in a commonwealth. For though it would be beside my present purpose to enter here into the particulars of the law of nature, or its measures of punishment, yet it is certain there is such a law, and that, too, as intelligible and plain to a rational creature and a studier of that law as the positive laws of commonwealths; nay, possibly plainer, as much as reason is easier to be understood than the fancies and intricate contrivances of men, following contrary and hidden interests put into words; for truly so are a great part of the municipal laws of countries, which are only so far right as they are founded on the law of nature, by which they are to be regulated and interpreted.

13. To this strange doctrine—viz., that in the state of nature everyone has the executive power of the law of nature—I doubt not but it will be objected that it is unreasonable for men to be judges in their own cases, that self-love will make men partial to themselves and their friends. And on the other side, that ill-nature, passion, and revenge will carry them too far in punishing others; and hence nothing but confusion and disorder will follow; and that therefore God hath certainly appointed government to restrain the partiality and violence of men. I easily grant that civil government is the proper remedy for the inconveniences of the state of nature, which must certainly be great where men may be judges in their own case, since 'tis easy to be imagined that he who was so unjust as to do his brother an injury, will scarce be so just as to condemn himself for it. But I shall desire those who make this objection, to remember that absolute monarchs are but men, and if government is to be the

remedy of those evils which necessarily follow from men's being judges in their own cases, and the state of nature is therefore not to be endured, I desire to know what kind of government that is, and how much better it is than the state of nature, where one man commanding a multitude, has the liberty to be judge in his own case, and may do to all his subjects whatever he pleases, without the least question or control of those who execute his pleasure; and in whatsoever he doth, whether led by reason, mistake, or passion, must be submitted to, which men in the state of nature are not bound to do one to another? And if he that judges, judges amiss in his own or any other case, he is answerable for it to the rest of mankind.

14. 'Tis often asked as a mighty objection, Where are, or ever were there, any men in such a state of nature? To which it may suffice as an answer at present: That since all princes and rulers of independent governments all through the world are in a state of nature, 'tis plain the world never was, nor ever will be, without numbers of men in that state. I have named all governors of independent communities, whether they are or are not in league with others. For 'tis not every compact that puts an end to the state of nature between men, but only this one of agreeing together mutually to enter into one community, and make one body politic; other promises and compacts men may make one with another, and yet still be in the state of nature. The promises and bargains for truck, etc., between the two men in Soldania, in or between a Swiss and an Indian, in the woods of America, are binding to them, though they are perfectly in a state of nature in reference to one another. For truth and keeping of faith belong to men as men, and not as members of society.

15. To those that say there were never any men in the state of nature, I will not only oppose the authority of the judicious Hooker—(Eccl. Pol., lib. i., sect. 10), where he says, "The laws which have been hitherto mentioned," i.e., the laws of nature, "do bind men absolutely, even as they are men, although they have never any settled fellowship, and never any solemn agreement amongst themselves what to do or not to do; but forasmuch as we are not by ourselves sufficient to furnish ourselves with competent store of things needful for such a life as our nature doth desire—a life fit for the dignity of man—therefore to supply those defects and imperfections which are in us, as living single and solely by ourselves, we are naturally induced to seek communion and fellowship with others; this was the cause of men's uniting themselves at first in politic societies"

—but I moreover affirm that all men are naturally in that state, and remain so, till by their own consents they make themselves members of some politic society; and I doubt not, in the sequel of this discourse, to make it very clear.

**Chapter V
Of Property**

25. Whether we consider natural reason, which tells us that men being once born have a right to their preservation, and consequently to meat and drink and such other things as nature affords for their subsistence; or revelation, which gives us an account of those grants God made of the world to Adam, and to Noah and his sons, 'tis very clear that God, as King David says, Psalm cxv. 16, "has given the earth to the children of men," given it to mankind in common. But this being supposed, it seems to some a very great difficulty how anyone should ever come to have a property in anything. I will not content myself to answer that if it be difficult to make out property upon a supposition that God gave the world to Adam and his posterity in common, it is impossible that any man but one universal monarch should have any property upon a supposition that God gave the world to Adam and his heirs in succession, exclusive of all the rest of his posterity. But I shall endeavor to show how men might come to have a property in several parts of that which God gave to mankind in common, and that without any express compact of all the commoners.

26. God, who hath given the world to men in common, hath also given them reason to make use of it to the best advantage of life and convenience. The earth and all that is therein is given to men for the support and comfort of their being. And though all the fruits it naturally produces, and beasts it feeds, belong to mankind in common, as they are produced by the spontaneous hand of nature; and nobody has originally a private dominion exclusive of the rest of mankind in any of them as they are thus in their natural state; yet being given for the use of men, there must of necessity be a means to appropriate them some way or other before they can be of any use or at all beneficial to any particular man. The fruit or venison which nourishes the wild Indian, who knows no enclosure, and is still a tenant in common, must be his, and so his, i.e., a part of him, that another can no longer have any right to it, before it can do any good for the support of his life.

27. Though the earth and all inferior creatures be common to all men, yet every man has a property in his own person; this

nobody has any right to but himself. The labor of his body and the work of his hands we may say are properly his. Whatsoever, then, he removes out of the state that nature hath provided and left it in, he hath mixed his labor with, and joined to it something that is his own, and thereby makes it his property. It being by him removed from the common state nature placed it in, it hath by this labor something annexed to it that excludes the common right of other men. For this labor being the unquestionable property of the laborer, no man but he can have a right to what that is once joined to, at least where there is enough, and as good left in common for others.

28. He that is nourished by the acorns he picked up under an oak, or the apples he gathered from the trees in the wood, has certainly appropriated them to himself. Nobody can deny but the nourishment is his. I ask, then, When did they begin to be his—when he digested, or when he ate, or when he boiled, or when he brought them home, or when he picked them up? And 'tis plain if the first gathering made them not his, nothing else could. That labor put a distinction between them and common; that added something to them more than nature, the common mother of all, had done, and so they became his private right. And will anyone say he had no right to those acorns or apples he thus appropriated, because he had not the consent of all mankind to make them his? Was it a robbery thus to assume to himself what belonged to all in common? If such a consent as that was necessary, man had starved, notwithstanding the plenty God had given him. We see in commons which remain so by compact that 'tis the taking any part of what is common and removing it out of the state nature leaves it in, which begins the property; without which the common is of no use. And the taking of this or that part does not depend on the express consent of all the commoners. Thus the grass my horse has bit, the turfs my servant has cut, and the ore I have dug in any place where I have a right to them in common with others, become my property without the assignation or consent of anybody. The labor that was mine removing them out of that common state they were in, hath fixed my property in them.

29. By making an explicit consent of every commoner necessary to anyone's appropriating to himself any part of what is given in common. Children or servants could not cut the meat which their father or master had provided for them in common without assigning to everyone his peculiar part. Though the water running in the fountain be everyone's, yet who can doubt but that in the pitcher is his only who drew it out? His labor

hath taken it out of the hands of Nature where it was common, and belonged equally to all her children, and hath thereby appropriated it to himself.

30. Thus this law of reason makes the deer that Indian's who hath killed it; it is allowed to be his goods who hath bestowed his labor upon it, though, before, it was the common right of everyone. And amongst those who are counted the civilized part of mankind, who have made and multiplied positive laws to determine property, this original law of nature for the beginning of property, in what was before common, still takes place, and by virtue thereof, what fish anyone catches in the ocean, that great and still remaining common of mankind; or what ambergris anyone takes up here is by the labor that removes it out of that common state nature left it in, made his property who takes that pains about it. And even amongst us, the hare that anyone is hunting is thought his who pursues her during the chase. For being a beast that is still looked upon as common, and no man's private possession, whoever has employed so much labor about any of that kind as to find and pursue her has thereby removed her from the state of nature wherein she was common, and hath began a property.

31. It will perhaps be objected to this, that if gathering the acorns, or other fruits of the earth, etc., makes a right to them, then anyone may engross as much as he will. To which I answer, Not so. The same law of nature that does by this means give us property, does also bound that property too. "God has given us all things richly" (1 Tim. vi. 17), is the voice of reason confirmed by inspiration. But how far has He given it us? To enjoy. As much as anyone can make use of to any advantage of life before it spoils, so much he may by his labor fix a property in; whatever is beyond this, is more than his share, and belongs to others. Nothing was made by God for man to spoil or destroy. And thus considering the plenty of natural provisions there was a long time in the world, and the few spenders, and to how small a part of that provision the industry of one man could extend itself, and engross it to the prejudice of others—especially keeping within the bounds, set by reason, of what might serve for his use—there could be then little room for quarrels or contentions about property so established.

32. But the chief matter of property being now not the fruits of the earth, and the beasts that subsist on it, but the earth itself, as that which takes in and carries with it all the rest, I think it is plain that property in that, too, is acquired as the former. As much land as a man tills, plants, improves, culti-

vates, and can use the product of, so much is his property. He by his labor does as it were enclose it from the common. Nor will it invalidate his right to say, everybody else has an equal title to it; and therefore he cannot appropriate, he cannot enclose, without the consent of all his fellow-commoners, all mankind. God, when He gave the world in common to all mankind, commanded man also to labor, and the penury of his condition required it of him. God and his reason commanded him to subdue the earth, i.e., improve it for the benefit of life, and therein lay out something upon it that was his own, his labor. He that, in obedience to this command of God, subdued, tilled, and sowed any part of it, thereby annexed to it something that was his property, which another had no title to, nor could without injury take from him.

33. Nor was this appropriation of any parcel of land, by improving it, any prejudice to any other man, since there was still enough and as good left; and more than the yet unprovided could use. So that in effect there was never the less left for others because of his enclosure for himself. For he that leaves as much as another can make use of, does as good as take nothing at all. Nobody could think himself injured by the drinking of another man, though he took a good draught, who had a whole river of the same water left him to quench his thirst; and the case of land and water, where there is enough of both, is perfectly the same.

34. God gave the world to men in common; but since He gave it them for their benefit, and the greatest conveniences of life they were capable to draw from it, it cannot be supposed He meant it, should always remain common and uncultivated. He gave it to the use of the industrious and rational (and labor was to be his title to it), not to the fancy or covetousness of the quarrelsome and contentious. He that had as good left for his improvement as was already taken up, needed not complain, ought not to meddle with what was already improved by another's labor; if he did, it is plain he desired the benefit of another's pains, which he had no right to, and not the ground which God had given him in common with others to labor on, and whereof there was as good left as that already possessed, and more than he knew what to do with, or his industry could reach to.

35. It is true, in land that is common in England, or any other country where there is plenty of people under Government, who have money and commerce, no one can enclose or appropriate any part without the consent of all his fellow-commoners: because this is left common by compact, i.e., by the law of

the land, which is not to be violated. And though it be common in respect of some men, it is not so to all mankind; but is the joint property of this country, or this parish. Besides, the remainder, after such enclosure, would not be as good to the rest of the commoners as the whole was, when they could all make use of the whole; whereas in the beginning and first peopling of the great common of the world it was quite otherwise. The law man was under was rather for appropriating. God commanded, and his wants forced him, to labor. That was his property, which could not be taken from him wherever he had fixed it. And hence subduing or cultivating the earth, and having dominion, we see are joined together. The one gave title to the other. So that God, by commanding to subdue, gave authority so far to appropriate. And the condition of human life, which requires labor and materials to work on, necessarily introduces private possessions.

36. The measure of property nature has well set by the extent of men's labor and the conveniency of life. No man's labor could subdue or appropriate all, nor could his enjoyment consume more than a small part; so that it was impossible for any man, this way, to entrench upon the right of another or acquire to himself a property to the prejudice of his neighbor, who would still have room for as good and as large a possession (after the other had taken out his) as before it was appropriated. Which measure did confine every man's possession to a very moderate proportion, and such as he might appropriate to himself without injury to anybody in the first ages of the world, when men were more in danger to be lost, by wandering from their company, in the then vast wilderness of the earth than to be straitened for want of room to plant in.

The same measure may be allowed still, without prejudice to anybody, full as the world seems. For, supposing a man or family, in the state they were at first, peopling of the world by the children of Adam or Noah, let him plant in some inland vacant places of America. We shall find that the possessions he could make himself, upon the measures we have given, would not be very large, nor, even to this day, prejudice the rest of mankind or give them reason to complain or think themselves injured by this man's encroachment, though the race of men have now spread themselves to all the corners of the world, and do infinitely exceed the small number was at the beginning. Nay, the extent of ground is of so little value without labor that I have heard it affirmed that in Spain itself a man may be permitted to plough, sow, and reap, without being disturbed, upon land he has no other title to, but only his making use of it. But, on the contrary, the inhabitants think themselves beholden to him who, by his industry on neglected, and consequently waste land, has increased the stock of corn, which they wanted. But be this as it will, which I lay no stress on, this I dare boldly affirm, that the same rule of propriety— viz., that every man should have as much as he could make use of, would hold still in the world, without straitening anybody, since there is land enough in the world to suffice double the inhabitants, had not the invention of money, and the tacit agreement of men to put a value on it, introduced (by consent) larger possessions and a right to them; which, how it has done, I shall by and by show more at large.

37. This is certain, that in the beginning, before the desire of having more than man needed had altered the intrinsic value of things, which depends only on their usefulness to the life of man; or had agreed that a little piece of yellow metal which would keep without wasting or decay should be worth a great piece of flesh or a whole heap of corn, though men had a right to appropriate by their labor, each one to himself, as much of the things of nature as he could use, yet this could not be much, nor to the prejudice of others, where the same plenty was still left to those who would use the same industry.

Before the appropriation of land, he who gathered as much of the wild fruit, killed, caught, or tamed as many of the beasts as he could; he that so employed his pains about any of the spontaneous products of nature as any way to alter them from the state which nature put them in, by placing any of his labor on them, did thereby acquire a propriety in them. But if they perished in his possession without their due use; if the fruits rotted, or the venison putrefied before he could spend it, he offended against the common law of nature, and was liable to be punished; he invaded his neighbor's share, for he had no right further than his use called for any of them and they might serve to afford him conveniences of life.

38. The same measures governed the possessions of land, too. Whatsoever he tilled and reaped, laid up, and made use of before it spoiled, that was his peculiar right; whatsoever he enclosed and could feed and make use of, the cattle and product was also his. But if either the grass of his enclosure rotted on the ground, or the fruit of his planting perished without gathering and laying up, this part of the earth, notwithstanding his enclosure, was still to be looked on as waste, and might be the possession of any other. Thus, at the beginning, Cain might take as much ground as he could till and make it his own land, and yet leave enough for Abel's sheep to feed on;

a few acres would serve for both their possessions. But as families increased, and industry enlarged their stocks, their possessions enlarged with the need of them; but yet it was commonly without any fixed property in the ground they made use of, till they incorporated, settled themselves together, and built cities; and then, by consent, they came in time to see out the bounds of their distinct territories, and agree on limits between them and their neighbors, and, by laws within themselves, settled the properties of those of the same society. For we see that in that part of the world which was first inhabited, and therefore like to be best peopled, even as low down as Abraham's time, they wandered with their flocks and their herds, which was their substance, freely up and down—and this Abraham did in a country where he was a stranger; whence it is plain that, at least, a great part of the land lay in common, that the inhabitants valued it not, nor claimed property in any more than they made use of; but when there was not room enough in the same place for their herds to feed together, they, by consent, as Abraham and Lot did (Gen. xiii. 5), separated and enlarged their pasture where it best liked them. And for the same reason, Esau went from his father and his brother, and planted in Mount Seir (Gen. xxxvi. 6).

39. And thus, without supposing any private dominion and property in Adam over all the world, exclusive of all other men, which can no way be proved, nor any one's property be made out from it, but supposing the world, given as it was to the children of men in common, we see how labor could make men distinct titles to several parcels of it for their private uses, wherein there could be no doubt of right, no room for quarrel.

40. Nor is it so strange, as perhaps before consideration it may appear, that the property of labor should be able to overbalance the community of land. For it is labor indeed that puts the difference of value on everything; and let anyone consider what the difference is between an acre of land planted with tobacco or sugar, sown with wheat or barley, and an acre of the same land lying in common without any husbandry upon it, and he will find that the improvement of labor makes the far greater part of the value. I think it will be but a very modest computation to say that of the products of the earth useful to the life of man nine-tenths are the effects of labor; nay, if we will rightly estimate things as they come to our use, and cast up the several expenses about them—what in them is purely owing to nature, and what to labor—we shall find that in most of them ninety-nine hundredths are wholly to be put on the account of labor.

41. There cannot be a clearer demonstration of anything than several nations of the Americans are of this, who are rich in land and poor in all the comforts of life; whom nature, having furnished as liberally as any other people with the materials of plenty—i.e., a fruitful soil, apt to produce in abundance what might serve for food, raiment, and delight; yet, for want of improving it by labor, have not one hundredth part of the conveniences we enjoy, and a king of a large and fruitful territory there feeds, lodges, and is clad worse than a day laborer in England.

42. To make this a little clearer, let us but trace some of the ordinary provisions of life, through their several progresses, before they come to our use, and see how much they receive of their value from human industry. Bread, wine, and cloth are things of daily use and great plenty; yet, notwithstanding, acorns, water, and leaves or skins, must be our bread, drink, and clothing, did not labor furnish us with these more useful commodities. For whatever bread is more worth than acorns, wine than water, and cloth or silk than leaves, skins, or moss, that is wholly owing to labor and industry: the one of these being the food and raiment which unassisted nature furnishes us with; the other, provisions which our industry and pains prepare for us; which how much they exceed the other in value when anyone hath computed, he will then see how much labor makes the far greatest part of the value of things we enjoy in this world. And the ground which produces the materials is scarce to be reckoned in as any, or at most but a very small, part of it; so little that even amongst us land that is left wholly to nature, that hath no improvement of pasturage, tillage, or planting, is called, as indeed it is, "waste," and we shall find the benefit of it amount to little more than nothing.

43. An acre of land that bears here twenty bushels of wheat, and another in America which, with the same husbandry, would do the like, are without doubt of the same natural intrinsic value; but yet the benefit mankind receives from the one in a year is worth £5, and from the other possibly not worth a penny, if all the profit an Indian received from it were to be valued and sold here; at least, I may truly say, not one-thousandth. 'Tis labor, then, which puts the greatest part of value upon land, without which it would scarcely be worth anything; 'tis to that we owe the greatest part of all its useful products, for all that the straw, bran, bread, of that acre of wheat is more worth than the product of an acre of as good land which lies waste, is all the effect of labor. For 'tis not barely the ploughman's pains, the reaper's and thresher's toil, and the baker's

sweat, is to be counted into the bread we eat; the labor of those who broke the oxen, who dug and wrought the iron and stones, who felled and framed the timber employed about the plough, mill, oven, or any other utensils, which are a vast number, requisite to this corn, from its sowing, to its being made bread, must all be charged on the account of labor, and received as an effect of that. Nature and the earth furnished only the almost worthless materials as in themselves. 'Twould be a strange catalogue of things that industry provided, and made use of, about every loaf of bread before it came to our use, if we could trace them—iron, wood, leather, bark, timber, stone, bricks, coals, lime, cloth, dyeing drugs, pitch, tar, masts, ropes, and all the materials made use of in the ship that brought any of the commodities made use of by any of the workmen to any part of the work all which it would be almost impossible—at least, too long—to reckon up.

44. From all which it is evident that, though the things of nature are given in common, yet man, by being master of himself and proprietor of his own person and the actions or labor of it, had still in himself the great foundation of property; and that which made up the great part of what he applied to the support or comfort of his being, when invention and arts had improved the conveniences of life, was perfectly his own, and did not belong in common to others.

45. Thus labor, in the beginning, gave a right of property, wherever anyone was pleased to employ it upon what was common, which remained a long while the far greater part, and is yet more than mankind makes use of. Men at first, for the most part, contented themselves with what unassisted nature offered to their necessities; and though afterwards, in some parts of the world (where the increase of people and stock, with the use of money, had made land scarce, and so of some value), the several communities settled the bounds of their distinct territories, and, by laws within themselves, regulated the properties of the private men of their society, and so, by compact and agreement, settled the property which labor and industry began—and the leagues that have been made between several states and kingdoms, either expressly or tacitly disowning all claim and right to the land in the other's posses- sion, have, by common consent, given up their pretenses to their natural common right, which originally they had to those countries; and so have, by positive agreement, settled a prop- erty amongst themselves in distinct parts of the world—yet there are still great tracts of ground to be found which, the inhabitants thereof not having joined with the rest of mankind

in the consent of the use of their common money, lie waste, and are more than the people who dwell on it do or can make use of, and so still lie in common; though this can scarce happen amongst that part of mankind that have consented to the use of money.

46. The greatest part of things really useful to the life of man, and such as the necessity of subsisting made the first commoners of the world look after, as it doth the Americans now are generally things of short duration, such as, if they are not consumed by use, will decay and perish of themselves: gold, silver, and diamonds are things that fancy or agreement have put the value on more than real use and the necessary support of life. Now, of those good things which nature hath provided in common, everyone hath a right, as hath been said, to as much as he could use, and had a property in all he could effect with his labor—all that his industry could extend to, to alter from the state nature had put it in, was his. He that gathered a hundred bushels of acorns or apples had thereby a property in them; they were his goods as soon as gathered. He was only to look that he used them before they spoiled, else he took more than his share, and robbed others; and, indeed, it was a foolish thing, as well as dishonest, to hoard up more than he could make use of. If he gave away a part to anybody else, so that it perished not uselessly in his possession, these he also made use of; and if he also bartered away plums that would have rotted in a week, for nuts that would last good for his eating a whole year, he did no injury; he wasted not the common stock, destroyed no part of the portion of goods that belonged to others, so long as nothing perished uselessly in his hands. Again, if he would give his nuts for a piece of metal, pleased with its color, or exchange his sheep for shells, or wool for a sparkling pebble or a diamond, and keep those by him all his life, he invaded not the right of others; he might heap up as much of these durable things as he pleased, the exceeding of the bounds of his just property not lying in the largeness of his possessions, but the perishing of anything uselessly in it.

47. And thus came in the use of money—some lasting thing that men might keep without spoiling, and that, by mutual consent, men would take in exchange for the truly useful but perishable supports of life.

48. And as different degrees of industry were apt to give men possessions in different proportions, so this invention of money gave them the opportunity to continue and enlarge them; for supposing an island, separate from all possible com-

merce with the rest of the world, wherein there were but a hundred families—but there were sheep, horses, and cows, with other useful animals, wholesome fruits, and land enough for corn for a hundred thousand times as many, but nothing in the island, either because of its commonness or perishableness, fit to supply the place of money—what reason could anyone have there to enlarge his possessions beyond the use of his family and a plentiful supply to its consumption, either in what their own industry produced, or they could barter for like perishable useful commodities with others? Where there is not something both lasting and scarce, and so valuable to be hoarded up, there men will not be apt to enlarge their possessions of land, were it never so rich, never so free for them to take; for I ask, what would a man value ten thousand or a hundred thousand acres of excellent land, ready cultivated, and well stocked too with cattle, in the middle of the inland parts of America, where he had no hopes of commerce with other parts of the world, to draw money to him by the sale of the product? It would not be worth the enclosing, and we should see him give up again to the wild common of nature whatever was more than would supply the conveniences of life to be had there for him and his family.

49. Thus in the beginning all the world was America, and more so than that is now, for no such thing as money was anywhere known. Find out something that hath the use and value of money amongst his neighbors, you shall see the same man will begin presently to enlarge his possessions.

50. But since gold and silver, being little useful to the life of man in proportion to food, raiment, and carriage, has its value only from the consent of men, whereof labor yet makes, in great part, the measure, it is plain that the consent of men have agreed to a disproportionate and unequal possession of the earth—I mean out of the bounds of society and compact; for in governments the laws regulate it; they having, by consent, found out and agreed in a way how a man may rightfully and without injury possess more than he himself can make use of by receiving gold and silver, which may continue long in a man's possession, without decaying for the overplus, and agreeing those metals should have a value.

51. And thus, I think, it is very easy to conceive without any difficulty how labor could at first begin a title of property in the common things of nature, and how the spending it upon our uses bounded it; so that there could then be no reason of quarrelling about title, nor any doubt about the largeness of possession it gave. Right and conveniency went together; for

as a man had a right to all he could employ his labor upon, so he had no temptation to labor for more than he could make use of. This left no room for controversy about the title, nor for encroachment on the right of others; what portion a man carved to himself was easily seen, and it was useless, as well as dishonest, to carve himself too much, or take more than he needed.

Jeremy Bentham

Anarchical Fallacies

Preliminary Observations

28 The Declaration of Rights—I mean the paper published under that name by the French National Assembly in 1791—assumes for its subject-matter a field of disquisition as unbounded in point of extent as it is important in its nature. But the more ample the extent given to any proposition or string of propositions, the more difficult it is to keep the import of it confined without deviation, within the bounds of truth and reason. If in the smallest corners of the field it ranges over, it fails of coinciding with the line of rigid rectitude, no sooner is the aberration pointed out, than (inasmuch as there is no medium between truth and falsehood) its pretensions to the appellation of a truism are gone, and whoever looks upon it must recognise it to be false and erroneous,—and if, as here, political conduct be the theme, so far as the error extends and fails of being detected, pernicious.

In a work of such extreme importance with a view to practice, and which throughout keeps practice so closely and immediately and professedly in view, a single error may be attended with the most fatal consequences. The more extensive the propositions, the more consummate will be the knowledge, the more exquisite the skill, indispensably requisite to confine them in all points within the pale of truth. The most consummate ability in the whole nation could not have been too much for the task—one may venture to say, it would not have been equal to it. But that, in the sanctioning of each proposition, the most consummate ability should happen to be vested in the heads of the sorry majority in whose hands the plenitude of power happened on that same occasion to be

The intellectual leader of the Radicals in England, Bentham (1748–1832) was an uncompromising utilitarian who played an important role in the political and social developments in his country. Among the important published works of Bentham are his *Principles of Morals and Legislation* (1789), *Theory of Legislation* (1802), and *Principles of the Constitutional Code* (1830, 1843). These selections are taken from Bentham's *Anarchical Fallacies*, Vol. 2 of the *Works*, ed. John Bowring, 1843.

vested, is an event against which the chances are almost as infinity to one.

Here, then, is a radical and all-pervading error—the attempting to give to a work on such a subject the sanction of government; especially of such a government—a government composed of members so numerous, so unequal in talent, as well as discordant in inclinations and affections. Had it been the work of a single hand, and that a private one, and in that character given to the world, every good effect would have been produced by it that could be produced by it when published as the work of government, without any of the bad effects which in case of the smallest error must result from it when given as the work of government.

The revolution, which threw the government into the hands of the penners and adopters of this declaration, having been the effect of insurrection, the grand object evidently is to justify the cause. But by justifying it, they invite it: in justifying past insurrection, they plant and cultivate a propensity to perpetual insurrection in time future; they sow the seeds of anarchy broad-cast: in justifying the demolition of existing authorities, they undermine all future ones, their own consequently in the number. Shallow and reckless vanity!—They imitate in their conduct the author of that fabled law, according to which the assassination of the prince upon the throne gave to the assassin a title to succeed him. *"People, behold your rights! If a single article of them be violated, insurrection is not your right only, but the most sacred of your duties."* Such is the constant language, for such is the professed object of this source and model of all laws—this self-consecrated oracle of all nations. . . .

. . . The great enemies of public peace are the selfish and dissocial passions:—necessary as they are—the one to the very existence of each individual, the other to his security. On the part of these affections, a deficiency in point of strength is never to be apprehended: all that is to be apprehended in respect of them, is to be apprehended on the side of their excess. Society is held together only by the sacrifices that men can be induced to make of the gratifications they demand: to obtain these sacrifices is the great difficulty, the great task of government. What has been the object, the perpetual and palpable object, of this declaration of pretended rights? To add as much force as possible to these passions, already but too strong,—to burst the cords that hold them in,—to say to the selfish passions, there—everywhere—is your prey!—to the angry passions, there—everywhere—is your enemy.

Such is the morality of this celebrated manifesto, rendered

famous by the same qualities that gave celebrity to the incendiary of the Ephesian temple.

The logic of it is of a piece with its morality:—a perpetual vein of nonsense, flowing from a perpetual abuse of words,—words having a variety of meanings, where words with single meanings were equally at hand—the same words used in a variety of meanings in the same page,—words used in meanings not their own, where proper words were equally at hand, —words and propositions of the most unbounded signification, turned loose without any of those exceptions or modifications which are so necessary on every occasion to reduce their import within the compass, not only of right reason, but even of the design in hand, of whatever nature it may be;—the same inaccuracy, the same inattention in the penning of this cluster of truths on which the fate of nations was to hang, as if it had been an oriental tale, or an allegory for a magazine:—stale epigrams, instead of necessary distinctions,—figurative expressions preferred to simple ones,—sentimental conceits, as trite as they are unmeaning, preferred to apt and precise expressions,—frippery ornament preferred to the majestic simplicity of good sound sense,—and the acts of the senate loaded and disfigured by the tinsel of the playhouse. . . .

Article II

The end in view of every political association is the preservation of the natural and imprescriptible rights of man. These rights are liberty, property, security, and resistance to oppression.

Sentence 1 The end in view of every political association, is the preservation of the natural and imprescriptible rights of man.

More confusion—more nonsense,—and the nonsense, as usual, dangerous nonsense. The words can scarcely be said to have a meaning: but if they have, or rather if they had a meaning, these would be the propositions either asserted or implied:—

1. *That there are such things as rights anterior to the establishment of governments: for natural, as applied to rights, if it mean anything, is meant to stand in opposition to* legal—*to such rights as are acknowledged to owe their existence to*

government, and are consequently posterior in their date to the establishment of government.

2. That these rights can not be abrogated by government: for can not is implied in the form of the word imprescriptible, and the sense it wears when so applied, is the cutthroat sense above explained.

3. That the governments that exist derive their origin from formal associations, or what are now called conventions: *associations entered into by a partnership contract, with all the members for partners,—entered into at a day prefixed, for a predetermined purpose, the formation of a new government where there was none before (for as to formal meetings holden under the control of an existing government, they are evidently out of question here) in which it seems again to be implied in the way of inference, though a necessary and an unavoidable inference, that all governments (that is, self-called governments, knots of persons exercising the powers of government) that have had any other origin than an association of the above description, are illegal, that is, no governments at all; resistance to them, and subversion of them, lawful and commendable; and so on.*

Such are the notions implied in this first part of the article. How stands the truth of things? That there are no such things as natural rights—no such things as rights anterior to the establishment of government—no such things as natural rights opposed to, in contradistinction to, legal: that the expression is merely figurative; that when used, in the moment you attempt to give it a literal meaning it leads to error, and to that sort of error that leads to mischief—to the extremity of mischief.

We know what it is for men to live without government—and living without government, to live without rights: we know what it is for men to live without government, for we see instances of such a way of life—we see it in many savage nations, or rather races of mankind; for instance, among the savages of New South Wales, whose way of living is so well known to us: no habit of obedience, and thence no government—no government, and thence no laws—no laws, and thence no such things as rights—no security—no property:—liberty, as against regular control, the control of laws and government—perfect; but as against all irregular control, the mandates of stronger individuals, none. In this state, at a time earlier than the commencement of history—in this same state, judging from analogy, we, the inhabitants of the part of the globe we call Europe, were;—no government, consequently no rights; no rights, consequently no property—no legal security—no legal liberty: security not more than belongs to beasts—forecast and sense of insecurity keener—consequently in point of happiness below the level of the brutal race.

In proportion to the want of happiness resulting from the want of rights, a reason exists for wishing that there were such things as rights. But reasons for wishing there were such things as rights, are not rights;—a reason for wishing that a certain right were established, is not that right—want is not supply—hunger is not bread.

That which has no existence cannot be destroyed—that which cannot be destroyed cannot require anything to preserve it from destruction. *Natural rights* is simple nonsense: natural and imprescriptible rights, rhetorical nonsense,—nonsense upon stilts. But this rhetorical nonsense ends in the old strain of mischievous nonsense: for immediately a list of these pretended natural rights is given, and those are so expressed as to present to view legal rights. And of these rights, whatever they are, there is not, it seems, any one of which any government *can,* upon any occasion whatever, abrogate the smallest particle.

So much for terrorist language. What is the language of reason and plain sense upon this same subject? That in proportion as it is *right* or *proper,* i.e. advantageous to the society in question, that this or that right—a right to this or that effect —should be established and maintained, in that same proportion it is *wrong* that it should be abrogated: but that as there is no *right,* which ought not to be maintained so long as it is upon the whole advantageous to the society that it should be maintained, so there is no right which, when the abolition of it is advantageous to society, should not be abolished. To know whether it would be more for the advantage of society that this or that right should be maintained or abolished, the time at which the question about maintaining or abolishing is proposed, must be given, and the circumstances under which it is proposed to maintain or abolish it; the right itself must be specifically described, not jumbled with an undistinguishable heap of others, under any such vague general terms as property, liberty, and the like.

One thing, in the midst of all this confusion, is but too plain. They know not of what they are talking under the name of natural rights, and yet they would have them imprescriptible— proof against all the power of the laws—pregnant with occasions summoning the members of the community to rise up in resistance against the laws. What, then, was their object in declaring the existence of imprescriptible rights, and without specifying a single one by any such mark as it could be known by? This and no other—to excite and keep up a spirit of resistance to all laws—a spirit of insurrection against all governments—against the governments of all other nations instantly,—against the government of their own nation—against the government they themselves were pretending to establish —even that, as soon as their own reign should be at an end. In us is the perfection of virtue and wisdom: in all mankind besides, the extremity of wickedness and folly. Our will shall consequently reign without control, and for ever: reign now we are living—reign after we are dead.

All nations—all future ages—shall be, for they are predestined to be, our slaves.

Future governments will not have honesty enough to be trusted with the determination of what rights shall be maintained, what abrogated—what laws kept in force, what repealed. Future subjects (I should say future citizens, for French government does not admit of subjects) will not have wit enough to be trusted with the choice whether to submit to the determination of the government of their time, or resist it. Governments, citizens—all to the end of time—all must be kept in chains.

Such are their maxims—such their premises—for it is by such premises only that the doctrine of imprescriptible rights and unrepealable laws can be supported.

What is the real source of these imprescriptible rights— these unrepealable laws? Power turned blind by looking from its own height: self-conceit and tyranny exalted into insanity. No man was to have any other man for a servant, yet all men were forever to be their slaves. Making laws with imposture in their mouths, under pretence of declaring them—giving for laws anything that came uppermost, and these unrepealable ones, on pretence of finding them ready made. Made by what? Not by a God—they allow of none; but by their goddess, Nature.

The origination of governments from a contract is a pure fiction, or in other words, a falsehood. It never has been known to be true in any instance; the allegation of it does mischief, by involving the subject in error and confusion, and is neither necessary nor useful to any good purpose.

All governments that we have any account of have been gradually established by habit, after having been formed by force; unless in the instance of governments formed by individuals who have been emancipated, or have emancipated themselves, from governments already formed, the governments under which they were born—a rare case, and from which nothing follows with regard to the rest. What signifies it how governments are formed? Is it the less proper—the less conducive to the happiness of society—that the happiness of society should be the one object kept in view by the members of the government in all their measures? Is it the less the interest of men to be happy—less to be wished that they may be so—less the moral duty of their governors to make them so, as far as they can, at Mogadore than at Philadelphia?

  Whence is it, but from government, that contracts derive their binding force? Contracts came from government, not government from contracts. It is from the habit of enforcing contracts, and seeing them enforced, that governments are chiefly indebted for whatever disposition they have to observe them.

Sentence 2   These rights [these imprescriptible as well as natural rights,] are liberty, property, security, and resistance to oppression.

  Observe the extent of these pretended rights, each of them belonging to every man, and all of them without bounds. Unbounded liberty; that is, amongst other things, the liberty of doing or not doing on every occasion whatever each man pleases:—Unbounded property; that is, the right of doing with everything around him (with every *thing* at least, if not with every person,) whatsoever he pleases; communicating that right to anybody, and withholding it from anybody:—Unbounded security; that is, security for such his liberty, for such his property, and for his person, against every defalcation that can be called for on any account in respect of any of them:— Unbounded resistance to oppression; that is, unbounded exercise of the faculty of guarding himself against whatever unpleasant circumstance may present itself to his imagination or his passions under that name. Nature, say some of the interpreters of the pretended law of nature—nature gave to each man a right to everything; which is, in effect, but another way of saying—nature has given no such right to anybody; for in regard to most rights, it is as true that what is every man's right is no man's right, as that what is every man's business is no man's business. Nature gave—gave to every man a right to everything:—be it so—true; and hence the necessity of human government and human laws, to give to every man his own right, without which no right whatsoever would amount to anything. Nature gave every man a right to everything before the existence of laws, and in default of laws. This nominal universality and real nonentity of right, set up provisionally by nature in default of laws, the French oracle lays hold of, and perpetuates it under the law and in spite of laws. These anarchical rights which nature had set out with, democratic art attempts to rivet down, and declares indefeasible.

Unbounded liberty—I must still say unbounded liberty;—for though the next article but one returns to the charge, and gives such a definition of liberty as seems intended to set bounds to it, yet in effect the limitation amounts to nothing; and when, as here, no warning is given of any exception in the texture of the general rule, every exception which turns up is, not a confirmation but a contradiction of the rule:—liberty, without any preannounced or intelligible bounds; and as to the other rights, they remain unbounded to the end: rights of man composed of a system of contradictions and impossibilities.

In vain would it be said, that though no bounds are here assigned to any of these rights, yet it is to be understood as taken for granted, and tacitly admitted and assumed, that they are to have bounds; viz. such bounds as it is understood will be set them by the laws. Vain, I say, would be this apology; for the supposition would be contradictory to the express declaration of the article itself, and would defeat the very object which the whole declaration has in view. It would be self-contradictory, because these rights are, in the same breath in which their existence is declared, declared to be imprescriptible; and imprescriptible, or, as we in England should say, indefeasible, means nothing unless it exclude the interference of the laws.

It would be not only inconsistent with itself, but inconsistent with the declared and sole object of the declaration, if it did not exclude the interference of the laws. It is against the laws themselves, and the laws only, that this declaration is levelled. It is for the hands of the legislator and all legislators, and none but legislators, that the shackles it provides are intended,—it is against the apprehended encroachments of legislators that the rights in question, the liberty and property, and so forth, are intended to be made secure,—it is to such encroachments, and damages, and dangers, that whatever security it professes to give has respect. Precious security for unbounded rights against legislators, if the extent of those rights in every direction were purposely left to depend upon the will and pleasure of those very legislators!

Nonsensical or nugatory, and in both cases mischievous: such is the alternative.

So much for all these pretended indefeasible rights in the

lump: their inconsistency with each other, as well as the inconsistency of them in the character of indefeasible rights with the existence of government and all peaceable society, will appear still more plainly when we examine them one by one.

1. *Liberty,* then, is imprescriptible—incapable of being taken away—out of the power of any government ever to take away: liberty,—that is, every branch of liberty—every individual exercise of liberty; for no line is drawn—no distinction—no exception made. What these instructors as well as governors of mankind appear not to know, is, that all rights are made at the expense of liberty—all laws by which rights are created or confirmed. No right without a correspondent obligation. Liberty, as against the coercion of the law, may, it is true, be given by the simple removal of the obligation by which that coercion was applied—by the simple repeal of the coercing law. But as against the coercion applicable by individual to individual, no liberty can be given to one man but in proportion as it is taken from another. All coercive laws, therefore (that is, all laws but constitutional laws, and laws repealing or modifying coercive laws,) and in particular all laws creative of liberty, are, as far as they go, abrogative of liberty. Not here and there a law only—not this or that possible law, but almost all laws, are therefore repugnant to these natural and imprescriptible rights: consequently null and void, calling for resistance and insurrection, and so on, as before.

Laws creative of rights of property are also struck at by the same anathema. How is property given? By restraining liberty; that is, by taking it away so far as is necessary for the purpose. How is your house made yours? By debarring every one else from the liberty of entering it without your leave.

2. *Property.* Property stands second on the list,—proprietary rights are in the number of the natural and imprescriptible rights of man—of the rights which a man is not indebted for to the laws, and which cannot be taken from him by the laws. Men —that is, every man (for a general expression given without exceptions is an universal one) has a right to property, to proprietary rights, *a right which* cannot be taken away from him by the laws. To proprietary rights. Good: but in relation to what subject? for as to proprietary rights—without a subject to which they are referable—without a subject in or in relation to which they can be exercised—they will hardly be of much value, they will hardly be worth taking care of, with so much solemnity. In vain would all the laws in the world have ascertained that I have a right to something. If this be all they have

done for me—if there be no specific subject in relation to which my proprietary rights are established, I must either take what I want without right, or starve. As there is no such subject specified with relation to each man, or to any man (indeed how could there be?) the necessary inference (taking the passage literally) is, that every man has all manner of proprietary rights with relation to every subject of property without exception: in a word, that every man has a right to every thing. Unfortunately, in most matters of property, what is every man's right is no man's right; so that the effect of this part of the oracle, if observed, would be, not to establish property, but to extinguish it—to render it impossible ever to be revived: and this is one of the rights declared to be imprescriptible.

It will probably be acknowledged, that according to this construction, the clause in question is equally ruinous and absurd:—and hence the inference may be, that this was not the construction—this was not the meaning in view. But by the same rule, every possible construction which the words employed can admit of, might be proved not to have been the meaning in view: nor is this clause a whit more absurd or ruinous than all that goes before it, and a great deal of what comes after it. And, in short, if this be not the meaning of it, what is? Give it a sense—give it any sense whatever,—it is mischievous:—to save it from that imputation, there is but one course to take, which is to acknowledge it to be nonsense.

Thus much would be clear, if anything were clear in it, that according to this clause, whatever proprietary rights, whatever property a man once has, no matter how, being imprescriptible, can never be taken away from him by any law: or of what use or meaning is the clause? So that the moment it is acknowledged in relation to any article, that such article is my property, no matter how or when it became so, that moment it is acknowledged that it can never be taken away from me: therefore, for example, all laws and all judgments, whereby anything is taken away from me without my free consent—all taxes, for example, and all fines—are void, and, as such, call for resistance and insurrection, and so forth, as before.

3. *Security.* Security stands the third on the list of these natural and imprescriptible rights which laws did not give, and which laws are not in any degree to be suffered to take away. Under the head of security, liberty might have been included, so likewise property: since security for liberty, or the enjoyment of liberty, may be spoken of as a branch of security:—security for property, or the enjoyment of proprietary rights, as

another. Security for person is the branch that seems here to have been understood:—security for each man's person, as against all those hurtful or disagreeable impressions (exclusive of those which consist in the mere disturbance of the enjoyment of liberty,) by which a man is affected in his person; loss of life—loss of limbs—loss of the use of limbs—wounds, bruises, and the like. All laws are null and void, then, which on any account or in any manner seek to expose the person of any man to any risk—which appoint capital or other corporal punishment—which expose a man to personal hazard in the service of the military power against foreign enemies, or in that of the judicial power against delinquents:—all laws which, to preserve the country from pestilence, authorize the immediate execution of a suspected person, in the event of his transgressing certain bounds.

4. *Resistance to oppression.* Fourth and last in the list of natural and imprescriptible rights, resistance to oppression—meaning, I suppose, the right to resist oppression. What is oppression? Power misapplied to the prejudice of some individual. What is it that a man has in view when he speaks of oppression? Some exertion of power which he looks upon as misapplied to the prejudice of some individual—to the producing on the part of such individual some suffering, to which (whether as forbidden by the laws or otherwise) we conceive he ought not to have been subjected. But against everything that can come under the name of oppression, provision has been already made, in the manner we have seen, by the recognition of the three preceding rights; since no oppression can fall upon a man which is not an infringement of his rights in relation to liberty, rights in relation to property, or rights in relation to security, as above described. Where, then, is the difference?—to what purpose this fourth clause after the three first? To this purpose: the mischief they seek to prevent, the rights they seek to establish, are the same; the difference lies in the nature of the remedy endeavoured to be applied. To prevent the mischief in question, the endeavour of the three former clauses is, to tie the hand of the legislator and his subordinates, by the fear of nullity, and the remote apprehension of general resistance and insurrection. The aim of this fourth clause is to raise the hand of the individual concerned to prevent the apprehended infraction of his rights at the moment when he looks upon it as about to take place.

Whenever you are about to be oppressed, you have a right to resist oppression: whenever you conceive yourself to be oppressed, conceive yourself to have a right to make resistance, and act accordingly. In proportion as a law of any kind—any act of power, supreme or subordinate, legislative, administrative, or judicial, is unpleasant to a man, especially if, in consideration of such its unpleasantness, his opinion is, that such act of power ought not to have been exercised, he of course looks upon it as oppression: as often as anything of this sort happens to a man—as often as anything happens to a man to inflame his passions,—this article, for fear his passions should not be sufficiently inflamed of themselves, sets itself to work to blow the flame, and urges him to resistance. Submit not to any decree or other act of power, of the justice of which you are not yourself perfectly convinced. If a constable call upon you to serve in the militia, shoot the constable and not the enemy; —if the commander of a press-gang trouble you, push him into the sea—if a bailiff, throw him out of the window. If a judge sentence you to be imprisoned or put to death, have a dagger ready, and take a stroke first at the judge.

Margaret Macdonald

Natural Rights

Doctrines of natural law and natural rights have a long and impressive history from the Stoics and Roman jurists to the Atlantic Charter and Roosevelt's Four Freedoms.[1] That men are entitled to make certain claims by virtue simply of their common humanity has been equally passionately defended and vehemently denied. Punctured by the cool scepticism of Hume; routed by the contempt of Bentham for 'nonsense upon stilts'; submerged by idealist and Marxist philosophers in the destiny of the totalitarian state; the claim to 'natural rights' has never been quite defeated. It tends in some form to be renewed in every crisis in human affairs, when the plain citizen tries to make, or expects his leaders to make, articulate his obscure, but firmly held, conviction that he is not a mere pawn in any political game, nor the property of any government or ruler, but the living and protesting individual for whose sake all political games are played and all governments instituted. As one of Cromwell's soldiers expressed it to that dictator: 'Really, sir, I think that the poorest he that is in England hath a life to live as the greatest he.'[2]

It could, perhaps, be proved hedonistically that life for most ordinary citizens is more *comfortable* in a democratic than a totalitarian state. But would an appeal for effort, on this ground, have been sanctioned between 1939–45? However true, it would have been rejected as inefficient because *uninspired*. Who could be moved to endure 'blood and toil, tears and sweat' for the sake of a little extra comfort? What, then, supplied the required inspiration? An appeal to the instinct of national self-preservation? But societies have been known to

Margaret Macdonald, late Reader in Philosophy, Bedford College, The University of London, was the author of a number of important philosophical essays on a wide range of topics. The essay on natural rights is an important contribution to the recent history of philosophical discussion of this topic. It appeared in *The Proceedings of The Aristotelian Society*, 1947–1948, and is reprinted here by courtesy of the Editor of The Aristotelian Society. Copyright 1947, The Aristotelian Society.

[1] Freedom of Speech and Worship; Freedom from Want and Fear of all persons everywhere.

[2] *Clarke Papers,* vol. 1, p. 301.

collapse inexplicably almost without waiting to be physically defeated. No doubt there are several answers, but at least one, I suggest, was an appeal to the values of freedom and equality among men. An appeal to safeguard and restore, where necessary, the Rights of Man, those ultimate points at which authority and social differences vanish, leaving the solitary individual with his essential human nature, according to one political theory, or a mere social fiction, according to another.

All this sounds very obscure. And the doctrine of natural law and of the natural rights of men is very obscure—which justifies the impatience of its opponents. It seems a strange law which is unwritten, has never been enacted, and may be unobserved without penalty, and peculiar rights which are possessed antecedently to all specific claims within an organized society. Surely, it will be said, the whole story now has only historical interest as an example of social mythology? Nothing is so dead as dead ideology. All this may be true,[3] but nevertheless the doctrine is puzzling. For if it is sheer nonsense why did it have psychological, political and legal effects? Men do not reflect and act upon collections of meaningless symbols or nonsense rhymes.

There seems no doubt that the assertions of certain Greek philosophers about the 'natural' equality of men and their consequent right to freedom caused intelligent contemporaries to become uneasy about the institution of slavery;[4] that doctrines of the primal Rights of Man were significantly connected with the French and American Revolutions. It even seems probable that the Communist Manifesto owed much of its success not to its 'scientific' analysis of capitalist society, but to its denouncement of a wage slavery degrading to human nature and its appeal to all workers to assert their equal brotherhood. A major crime of capitalist society for Marx and Engels was that it had destroyed all ties between men other than naked self-interest and had 'resolved personal worth into exchange value.' Only after the proletarian revolution would *human* history begin and men treat each other as equal human beings, not as exploiter and exploited. The object of the transfer of class power is to end class power and to reveal or restore some essential human nature at present disguised by distorting social relationships.

So even if the theory were dead, the puzzle of its effects

---

[3] It is not quite true, for the doctrines of natural law and consequent natural rights flourish in Catholic social philosophy. See e.g. *The Rights of Man and Natural Law* by Jacques Maritain; 1944.

[4] Cf. *The Open Society*, by K. Popper; vol. 1, esp. pp. 58–9.

would remain, and suggest that it had been introduced to solve a genuine problem of political and social philosophy. And it is interesting, therefore, to inquire what the problem was; whether it has found an alternative solution, or is bogus and insoluble.

Why should people have supposed, and, as I believe, continue to suppose, in obscure fashion, that they have 'natural' rights, or rights as human beings, independently of the laws and governments of any existing society? It is, surely, partly at least, because no existing social compulsion or relationship is self-justifying. Men may always ask why they should or should not endure it and expect a convincing answer. And, ultimately, it would seem, they may challenge the dictates of all existing governments and the pressures of every society if they find them equally oppressive, i.e. if they deny what the individual considers his fundamental 'right.' But since, *ex hypothesi,* this 'right' is denied by every existing law and authority, it must be a right possessed independently of them and derived from another source. If, e.g., the laws of every existing society condemn a human being to be a slave, he, or another on his behalf, may yet hold that he has a 'right' to be free. What sort of proposition is this and how is such a claim to be justified? This seems to be one most important problem which the doctrine of natural rights tried to solve.

Natural Law, Natural Laws, and Natural Rights

There are an indefinite number of different types of propositions and other forms of human utterance. I will, for my present purpose, notice three. (1) Tautological or analytic propositions which state rules for the uses of symbols or which follow from such rules within a linguistic or logical system. (2) Empirical or contingent propositions which state matter of fact and existence. Propositions which describe what does or may occur in the world and not the symbolic techniques employed in such description. (3) Assertions or expressions of value. With the help of this classification it may be possible to show that some of the difficulties of the doctrine of natural rights have been due to an attempt to interpret propositions about natural rights as a curious hybrid of types (1) and (2) of the above classification.

For in the theory which conceived of natural rights as guaranteed by a 'natural' law, the position seems to have been considered in the following terms. The 'rights' of a slave, e.g.

derive from the laws in any society which govern his artificial status as a slave. Yet he has a right to be free. But in virtue of what status and law? Only it seems by his status of being a man like other men. This, however, is a natural status as opposed to one determined by social convention. Every man is human 'by nature'; no human being is 'by nature' a slave of another human being. There must then be an essential human nature which determines this status and a law governing the relations of human beings as such, independently of the laws of all particular societies concerning their artificial relationships. But essential human nature or human 'essence' is constituted by those properties expressed in the definition of 'human being.' And what is expressed or entailed by a definition is a necessary or analytic proposition. Thus by a logical fusion of the characteristics of two different types of proposition, statements about natural rights tended in this theory to be represented as statements of a necessary natural fact.

But not even statements of actual fact, necessary or contingent. For another element intervened. Though the slave had an actual 'right' to be free, he was not free, because no existing law admitted his right. Because laws were imperfect, he was not free though he 'ought' to be. And this introduces into the situation a further complication. By nature a man must be that which yet he is not. Or, it follows from the definition of 'human being' that every human being is, or must be, free—or possess any other 'natural' right though his freedom is ideal and not real. But the ideal as well as the actual is natural fact.

Thus the Roman lawyers, who gave the earliest authoritative statements of the doctrine of natural law, conceived of natural law as an ideal or standard, not yet completely exemplified in any existing legal code, but also as a standard fixed by nature to be discovered and gradually applied by men. And the good lawyer kept his eye on this standard as the good gardener keeps his eye fixed on the prize rose which he is hoping to reproduce among his own blooms next summer. For the lawyer, said Ulpian, is not merely the interpreter of existing laws but also the priest or guardian of justice, which is the 'fixed and abiding disposition to give every man his right.'[5] This standard was not determined by men, but by nature, or, sometimes, by God. It was fact and not fancy.

The institution of slavery showed that no existing code was perfectly just. Thus natural *law* is only imperfectly realized in positive *laws*. And it is significant that the lawyers and later

---

[5] Sabine: *History of Political Theory*, p. 170.

political theorists who adopted this distinction talked only of natural *law* and *the* Law of Nature, never of natural laws and laws of nature. But what is most characteristic of legal codes and systems is that they consist of many laws, regulating the different relations of men as debtor and creditor, property owner and thief, employer and employee, husband and wife, etc. But natural law was not conceived of as consisting of ideal regulations corresponding to all positive laws. Indeed, if completely realized, some positive laws would be abolished, e.g. those relating to slave owner and slave. Natural law was not formulated in natural *laws.* It was neither written nor customary and might even be unknown. But it applies, nevertheless, to all men everywhere whether they are debtors or creditors, masters or servants, bond or free. But how is it discovered?

It seems probable that the concept of natural law influenced the later conception of natural or scientific laws obtained by the observation of natural events. For natural law applies impartially to all men in all circumstances, as the law of gravitation applies to all bodies. But the law of gravitation is obtained by deduction from the observation of bodies in sense perception. Are the Law of Nature and the Rights which it implies known by similar observation of the nature of man? The law of gravitation, like all other laws of nature, states a uniformity exemplified in the actual movements of natural bodies. But no existing society may observe the Law of Nature or guarantee natural rights. These cannot, therefore, have been learned from observation of the actual practice of existing societies.

'Man is born free,' said Rousseau, 'and everywhere he is in chains.' What sort of proposition is this? Did Rousseau observe ten or ten million babies immediately after birth and record when the infant limbs were manacled? The law of nature applies to all men equally, said Cicero. For if we had not been corrupted by bad habits and customs 'no one would be so like his own self as all men would be like others.'[6] But since everyone everywhere has been subjected to customs and laws of varying degrees of imperfection, where and when did Cicero observe our uncorrupted nature? How can facts about nature be discovered which have never been observed or confirmed by observation?

The answer lies in the peculiar status given to reason in the theory. Propositions about natural law and natural rights are not generalizations from experience nor deductions from observed facts subsequently confirmed by experience. Yet they

[6] *Laws,* Bk. 1, 10, 28–9 (trans. C. W. Keyes).

are not totally disconnected from natural fact. For they are known as entailed by the intrinsic or essential nature of man. Thus they are known by reason. But they are entailed by the proposition that an essential property of men is that they have reason. The standard of natural law is set by reason and is known because men have reason. But that men have reason, i.e. are able to deduce the ideal from the actual, is a natural fact. And it is by having this specific, and natural, characteristic of being rational that men resemble each other and differ from the brutes. Reason is the great leveller or elevator. According to Sir Frederick Pollock, 'Natural law was conceived to be an ultimate principle of fitness with regard to the nature of man as a rational and social being which is, or ought to be, the justification of every form of positive law.'[7] 'There is, in fact,' said Cicero, 'a true law—namely right reason—which is in accordance with nature, applies to all men and is unchangeable and eternal.'[8] And for Grotius, too, 'The law of nature is a dictate of right reason.'[9]

Let it be admitted that all or most human beings are intelligent or rational. And that what is known by reason is certainly true. But, also, what can be known by unaided reason is what *must* be true, and perhaps what *ought* to be but never what *is* true of matter of fact. And statements which are logically certain are tautological or analytic and are neither verified nor falsified by what exists. Statements about what ought to be are of a peculiar type which will be discussed later, but it is certain that they say nothing about what *is.* Because it is confused on these distinctions, the theory of natural law and natural rights constantly confounds reason with right and both with matter of fact and existence. The fact that men do reason is thought to be somehow a natural or empirical confirmation of what is logically deduced by reason as a standard by which to judge the imperfections of what exists.

The Social Contract

Though the Roman lawyers conceded that a man might be entitled by natural law to that which he was denied by every positive law, they do not seem to have related this to any particular doctrine of legal and political authority. But in the seventeenth century the doctrines of natural law and natural

---

[7] The History of the Law of Nature; *Essays in the Law,* 1922.
[8] *Republic,* Bk. 3, p. 22 (trans. Sabine and Smith).
[9] Bk. 1, ch. 1, sec. x, 1.

rights were directly connected with the contract theory of the State. Because he is rational, Locke emphasized, man is subject to the law of nature even before the establishment of civil society. And he never ceases to be so subject. By right of the law of nature men lived in a state of freedom, equality and the possession of property 'that with which a man hath mixed his labour.' True, this picture differs from that of Hobbes whose 'natural man' is constantly at war, possesses only the right to preserve his life, if he can, but usually finds it short and nasty. Nevertheless, even Hobbes's unpleasant savages have sufficient sense, or reason, to enable them to escape their 'natural' predicament. Locke's natural individualists are peaceful property owners who nevertheless sometimes dispute and want an impartial arbitrator. Civil society is formed by compact that natural rights may be better preserved. Man did not enter society, said Paine, to become *worse* than he was before by surrendering his natural rights but only to have them better secured. His natural rights are the foundation of all his civil rights. It was essential for the social contract theorists to deny that all rights are the gift of civil society, since existing societies denied certain rights which they affirmed. In order to claim them, therefore, it was supposed that they had been enjoyed or were such as would be enjoyed by rational creatures in a 'natural' as opposed to an established society. The Declaration of the French Revolutionary Assembly enunciated the Rights of Man and of citizens; the two being distinct.

His 'natural' rights attach, by virtue of his reason, to every man much as do his arms and legs. He carries them about with him from one society to another. He cannot lose them without losing himself. 'Men are born free and equal,' said the French Assembly, 'in respect of their *natural* and *imprescriptible* rights of liberty, property, security and resistance of oppression.' The framers of the American Declaration of Independence declare as self-evident truths that all men are created equal, that they are endowed by their creator with certain inalienable rights, among which are Life, Liberty and the Pursuit of Happiness and that governments are instituted to secure these rights. The free people of Virginia proclaimed that the rights with which men enter society they cannot by any compact deprive themselves or their posterity.

These were self-evident truths about a state which men might have left or not yet attained but which was 'natural' to them as opposed to accidental or conventional. A person is accidentally a native of England, France, America; a Red Indian, negro or Jew. His social environment is determined by accident of birth. He may change his family by adoption and his citizenship by naturalization. And he is accidentally, or conventionally, a doctor, soldier, employer, etc. These conventionalities determine his civic and legal rights in a particular society. But he is not accidentally human. Humanity is his essence or nature. There is no essence of 'being Greek' or 'being English'; of 'being a creditor' or 'being an old age pensioner' all of which properties, however, might be the basis of civil rights. The nature of man determines his 'natural' rights. And since, though not accidental, it also seemed to be a matter of fact that men exist and are rational, rights claimed on account of this fact seemed also to be natural and to follow from the essence of man, even though they might be denied. But the essence of man is expressed in the definition of the word 'man.' So that the statement 'Men have natural rights' is equivalent to the propositional function 'x is human entails x had natural rights' which is a tautology. Again the ambiguity inherent in the theory between what is necessary and what is natural, is revealed. It is hard to believe that a barren tautology generated the ardours of that time in which it was good to be alive and to be young was 'very heaven.'[10] But what is meant by the nature or essence of man by 'being rational' or 'having reason'?

Rights and Reason

" 'Man' equals 'rational animal' Df." is the fossil preserved in logic text books since Aristotle. It was never accompanied by any adequate account of the meaning of 'rational' which· was, however, generally assumed to include the capacity to abstract and generalize by the use of symbols in speech and writing; to formulate and understand general propositions and laws and to perceive necessary or logical connections between propositions. It is true that Aristotle himself used the term 'reason' more widely to include the practical intelligence manifested in various skills and the appropriate behaviour of the well-trained character in various moral situations. But usually reason is conceived to be the capacity by which men understand abstractions. This was certainly Kant's view. To be rational is to be able to think abstractly. And the most characteristic activities of men, including living in societies, are due to this capacity to use reason. It is peculiar to men and shared by no other animal. Hence the basis of the equality of men for the expo-

---

[10] Wordsworth in *The French Revolution.*

nents of natural law, and of their intrinsic worth for Kant is the fact that they all have reason. Men share all other characteristics with the brutes and might themselves have them in varying degrees, but reason was alike in all men, it was man's defining characteristic. Hence it is the foundation, too, of his natural rights, as a human being.

It is probable that other animals do not abstract and generalize for they do not use symbols. But neither is it true that all men do this with equal skill. Reason, in this sense, is no less or no more invariable among human beings than sense perception, and the rights of man might as well depend upon eyesight as upon rationality. But if the term reason is to be used more widely to include non-verbal manifestations of intelligence, knowing-how as well as knowing-that,[11] then intelligence does not set an unbridgeable gulf between men and other living creatures. For in many activities, those, i.e., of hunting, building, fighting, and even social organization, other creatures display skill, adaptability of means to ends, and other characteristics which are evidence of intelligence in men. And as for social life, ants use tools, domesticate other insects, and live a highly organized social life. Bees and wasps manage their affairs by a complicated system of government. Moreover, many of the most characteristic human activities depend very little on abstract thought or use of symbols, e.g. cooking, sewing, knitting, carpentry. And at a higher level the excellence of pictures, sculptures, symphonies, is not due to their expression of abstract thought. But where in this variety are we to find the constant factor by which to determine human rights? What passport will admit to the Kingdom of Ends?

What may be agreed is that only at a certain level of intellectual development do men claim natural rights. Savages do not dream of life, liberty and the pursuit of happiness. For they do not question what is customary. Neither do the very depressed and downtrodden. It was not the slaves who acclaimed their right to be free but the philosophers and lawyers. Marx and Engels were not themselves wage slaves of the industrial system. It is generally agreed that the doctrines of natural rights, natural law and the social contract, are individualistic. To claim rights as an individual independently of society, a man must have reached a level of self-consciousness which enables him to isolate himself in thought from his social environment. This presupposes a considerable capacity for ab-

---

[11] See Presidential Address to the Aristotelian Society by Professor G. Ryle, 1945, and *The Concept of Mind,* 1949, ch. II.

straction. To this extent natural rights, or the ability to claim natural rights, depends on reason. But it does not follow from this that reason alone constitutes the specific nature of man or that the worth of human beings is determined solely by their I.Q.s. Reason is only one human excellence.

But the Aristotelian dream of fixed natures pursuing common ends dies hard. It reappears in M. Maritain's account of the Rights of Man cited earlier. He says, e.g.:

. . . there is a human nature and this human nature is the same in all men . . . and possessed of a nature, constituted in a given determinate fashion, man obviously possesses ends which correspond to his natural constitution and which are the same for all—as all pianos, for instance, whatever their particular type and in whatever spot they may be, have as their end the production of certain attuned sounds. If they do not produce these sounds, they must be attuned or discarded as worthless . . . since man has intelligence and can determine his ends, it is up to him to put himself in tune with the ends necessarily demanded by his nature.[12]

And men's rights depend upon this common nature and end by which they are subject to the natural or 'unwritten' law. But this seems to me a complete mistake. Human beings are not like exactly similar bottles of whisky each marked 'for export only' or some device indicating a common destination or end. Men do not share a fixed nature, nor, therefore, are there any ends which they must necessarily pursue in fulfilment of such nature. There is no definition of 'man.' There is a more or less vague set of properties which characterize in varying degrees and proportions those creatures which are called 'human.' These determine for each individual human being what he *can* do but not what he *must* do. If he has an I.Q. of 85 his intellectual activities will be limited; if he is physically weak he cannot become a heavyweight boxer. If a woman has neither good looks nor acting ability she is unlikely to succeed as a film star. But what people may do with their capacities is extremely varied, and there is no one thing which they must do in order to be human. It would be nonsense to say: 'I am not going to be an actress, a school teacher, a postman, a soldier, a taxpayer, but simply a human being.' For what is the alternative? A man may choose whether he will become a civil servant or a schoolmaster; a conservative or a socialist, but he cannot

[12] *Loc. cit.*, p. 35.

choose whether he will be a man or a dog. There is certainly a sense in which it is often said that in the air-raid shelter or in the battle people forgot that they were officers or privates, assistant secretaries or typists, rich or poor, and remembered only that they were all human beings, i.e. all liable to die without regard to status. But that is always true. They did not remember that they were something *in addition* to being the particular human being they each were and which they might be without being any particular individual. And, as individuals, when the 'All Clear' sounded, each returned to pursue his or her own ends, not the purpose of the human race. Certainly, many human beings may co-operate in a joint enterprise to achieve a particular end which each chooses. But that cannot be generalized into the spectacle of all human beings pursuing one end. There is no end set for the human race by an abstraction called 'human nature.' There are only ends which individuals choose, or are forced by circumstances to accept. There are none which they *must* accept. Men are not created for a purpose as a piano is built to produce certain sounds. Or if they are we have no idea of the purpose.

It is the emphasis on the individual sufferer from bad social conditions which constitutes the appeal of the social contract theory and the 'natural' origin of human rights. But it does not follow that the theory is true as a statement of verifiable fact about the actual constitution of the world. The statements of the Law of Nature are not statements of the laws of nature, not even of the laws of an 'ideal' nature. For nature provides no standards or ideals. All that exists, exists at the same level, or is of the same logical type. There are not, by nature, prize roses, works of art, oppressed or unoppressed citizens. Standards are determined by human choice, not set by nature independently of men. Natural events cannot tell us what we ought to do until we have made certain decisions, when knowledge of natural fact will enable the most efficient means to be chosen to carry out those decisions. Natural events themselves have no value, and human beings as natural existents have no value either, whether on account of possessing intelligence or having two feet.

One of the major criticisms of the doctrine of natural rights is that the list of natural rights varies with each exponent. For Hobbes, man's only natural right is self-preservation. More 'liberal' theorists add to life and security; liberty, the pursuit of happiness and sometimes property. Modern socialists would probably include the right to 'work or adequate maintenance.' M. Maritain enumerates a list of nine natural rights which include besides the rights to life, liberty, and property of the older formulations, the right to pursue a religious vocation, the right to marry and raise a family, and, finally, the right of every human being to be treated as a person and not as a thing.[13] It is evident that these 'rights' are of very different types which would need to be distinguished in a complete discussion of the problem. My aim in this paper, however, is only to try to understand what can be meant by the assertion that there are some rights to which human beings are entitled independently of their varying social relationships. And it seems difficult to account for the wide variations in the lists of these 'rights' if they have all been deduced from a fixed human nature or essence, subject to an absolutely uniform 'natural law.' Nor is the disagreement one which can be settled by more careful empirical observation of human beings and their legal systems. The doctrine seems to try to operate by an analogy which it is logically impossible to apply.

The word 'right' has a variety of uses in ordinary language, which include the distinction between 'legal right' and 'moral right.' 'A has a legal right against B' entails B has a duty to A which will be enforced by the courts. A has a claim against B recognized by an existing law. No person has a legal right which he cannot claim from some other (legal) person and which the law will not enforce. That A has a moral right against B likewise entails that B has a duty to A. But it is not necessarily a duty which can be legally enforced. A has a right to be told the truth by B and B has a corresponding duty to tell A the truth. But no one, except in special circumstances recognized by law, can force B to tell the truth, or penalize him, except by censure, if he does not. No one can, in general, claim to be told the truth, by right, under penalty. But a creditor can claim repayment of a debt or sue his debtor.

When the lawyers said that a slave had a right in natural law to be free, they thought of a legal right not provided for by any existing statute, enactment or custom and to whose universal infringement no penalties attached. But this, surely, is the vanishing point of law and of legal right? It indicates that there just wasn't a law or legal right by which a slave might demand his freedom. But perhaps there was a moral right and a moral obligation. The slave ought to be free and maybe it was the duty of every slaveholder to free his slaves and of legislators to enact laws forbidding slavery. But until this happened there was no law which forbade a man to keep slaves. Consequently,

---

[13] *Loc. cit.*, p. 60.

there is no point in saying there was 'really' a natural law which forbade this. For the natural law was impotent. Statements about natural law were neither statements of natural fact nor legal practice.

So, does it follow that a 'natural' right is just a 'moral' right? Kant said, in effect, that to treat another human being as a person, of intrinsic worth, an end in himself, is just to treat him in accordance with the moral law applicable to all rational beings on account of their having reason. But this is not quite the sense in which the term 'natural rights' has been historically used. Declarations of the Rights of Man did not include his right to be told the truth, to have promises kept which had been made to him, to receive gratitude from those he had benefited, etc. The common thread among the variety of natural rights is their *political* character. Despite their rugged individualism, no exponent of the Rights of Man desired to enjoy them, in solitude, on a desert island. They were among the articles of the original Social Contract; clauses in Constitutions, the inspiration of social and governmental reforms. But 'Keep promises'; 'Tell the truth'; 'Be grateful' are not inscribed on banners carried by aggrieved demonstrators or circulated among the members of an oppressed party. Whether or not morality can exist without society, it is certain that politics cannot. Why then were 'natural rights' conceived to exist independently of organized society and hence of political controversies? I suggest that they were so considered in order to emphasize their basic or fundamental character. For words like freedom, equality, security, represented for the defenders of natural rights what they considered to be the fundamental moral and social values which should be or should continue to be realized in any society fit for intelligent and responsible citizens.

When the contract theorists talked of the rights of human beings which men had enjoyed in the state of nature, they seemed to be asserting unverifiable and nonsensical propositions since there is no evidence of a state of nature in which men lived before the establishment of civil societies. But they were not simply talking nonsense. They were, in effect, saying 'In any society and under every form of government men ought to be able to think and express their thoughts freely; to live their lives without arbitrary molestation with their persons and goods. They ought to be treated as equal in value, though not necessarily of equal capacity or merit. They ought to be assured of the exclusive use of at least some material objects other than their own bodies; they ought not to be governed without some form of consent. And that the application of these rights to the particular conditions of a society, or their suspension, if necessary, should be agreed with them.' The exponents of the natural Rights of Man were trying to express what they deemed to be the fundamental conditions of *human* social life and government. And it is by the observance of some such conditions, I suggest, that human societies are distinguished from ant hills and beehives.

This, however, has frequently been denied by utilitarian, idealist and marxist philosophers who, though differing in other respects, agree in holding that the rights of an individual must be determined only by the needs and conveniences of society as a whole. Surely, they say, there can be no 'natural' right to life in any society when a man may be executed as a criminal or killed as a conscripted soldier. And very little right to liberty exists when external danger threatens the state. 'The person with rights and duties,' says the evolutionist utilitarian Ritchie, 'is the product of society and the rights of the individual must, therefore, be judged from the point of view of society as a whole and not the society from the point of view of the individual.'[14] It is the duty of the individual to preserve society for his descendants. For individuals perish but England remains. But the plain man may well ask why he must preserve a society for his descendants if it neither is, nor shows any prospect of being, worth living in? Will his descendants thank him for this consideration? All that seems to follow from Ritchie's view is that at any time the members of a society may agree to sacrifice some goods in order to achieve a certain result. And the result will include the restoration of basic rights. Does the ordinary citizen consider that he has no right to life and liberty because he agrees to (or does not protest against) the suspension of those rights in an emergency? He would be very unlikely to approve of such suspension if he thought the result would be the massacre or enslavement of himself, his contemporaries and possibly his children and descendants at the arbitrary will of a ruler or government. To suspend, or even to forfeit rights, as a criminal does, also temporarily, is not to deny rights. Nor is it to deny that such practices must be justified to the individuals required to submit to them. Though it may be much more useful to society that a man should remain a slave and even that he may be happier in that condition, it is not possible to prove to him that he has no right to be free, however much society wants his slavery. In short,

---

[14] Ritchie: *Natural Rights,* p. 101.

'natural rights' are the conditions of a good society. But what those conditions are is not given by nature or mystically bound up with the essence of man and his inevitable goal, but is determined by human decisions.

Propositions and Decisions

Assertions about natural rights, then, are assertions of what ought to be as the result of human choice. They fall within class 3 of the division stated on page 42, as being ethical assertions or expressions of value. And these assertions or expressions include all those which result from human choice and preference, in art and personal relations, e.g. as well as in morals and politics. Such utterances in which human beings express choices determined by evaluation of better and worse have been variously interpreted, and it is, indeed, difficult to introduce a discussion of the topic without assuming an interpretation. I have tried, e.g. to avoid the use of the words 'proposition' and 'statement' in referring to these utterances since these words emphasize a relation between what is asserted and a fact by which it is verified or falsified. And this leads either to the attempts of the natural law and natural rights theories to find a 'natural' fact which justifies these assertions or to a search for non-sensible entities called 'Values' as the reference of ethical terms. Yet, of course, it is, in some sense, true that 'No one ought to be ill-treated because he is a Jew, a negro or not able to count above ten.' Alternatively, to talk of 'expressions of value' sounds as though such utterances are sophisticated ways of cheering and cursing. Just as the blow becomes sublimated into the sarcastic retort so our smiles of delight at unselfish action and howls of woe at parricide become intellectualized into apparent judgments about good and evil, right and wrong, without, however, losing their fundamentally emotive character.[15] On this view, value judgments do not state what is true or false but are expressions of feeling, sometimes combined with commands to do or forbear. But whatever its emotional causes and effects, an articulate utterance does not seem to be simply a substitute for a smile or a tear. It says something. But I cannot hope in a necessarily brief discussion to do justice to the enormous variety of value utterances. So I will plunge, and say that value utterances are more like records of *decisions* than proposi-

[15] Cf. A. J. Ayer: *Language, Truth and Logic,* ch. 6.

tions.[16] To assert that 'Freedom is better than slavery' or 'All men are of equal worth' is not to state a fact but to *choose a side*. It announces *This is where I stand*.

I mentioned earlier that in the late war propaganda appeals to defend our comforts and privileges would have been rejected as uninspiring but that appeals to defend the rights of all men to freedom and equality obtained the required response, at least in all but the depraved and cynical. I now suggest that they did so because they accorded with our decisions about these ultimate social values. For whether or not we were more or less comfortable as a result, we should not choose to act only upon orders about which we had not in some way been consulted; to suppress the truth; to imprison without trial or to permit human individuals or classes of individuals to be treated as of no human value.

Two questions suggest themselves on this view. Firstly, if ethical judgments, and particularly the ethical judgments which concern the fundamental structure of society are value decisions, who makes these decisions and when? Is this not, as much as the natural law theory, the use of an analogy without application? I did safeguard myself to some extent by saying that these assertions are 'more like' decisions than they are like propositions. They are unlike propositions because they are neither tautologies nor statements of verifiable fact. But it is also true that if asked when we decided in favour of free speech or democratic government or many of our social values we could not give a date. It is, therefore, suggested that we no more record a decision by a value assertion than we signed a Social Contract. Nevertheless, I think the analogy does emphasize important differences between value and other assertions. For, if intelligent, we do choose our politics as we choose our friends or our favoured poems, novels, pictures, symphonies, and as we do not choose to accept Pythagoras's theorem or the law of gravitation. And when challenged we affirm our decision or stand by our choice. We say, 'I did not realize how much I valued free speech until I went to Germany in 1936,' indicating that a choice had been made, but so easily that it had seemed scarcely necessary to record its occurrence.

For, indeed, the fundamental values of a society are not always recorded in explicit decisions by its members, even its rulers, but are expressed in the life of the society and consti-

---

[16] Dr. K. R. Popper makes a similar distinction in an interesting discussion of value judgments in *The Open Society*, vol. 1, ch. 5.

tute its quality. They are conveyed by its 'tone' and atmosphere as well as its laws and Statutory Rules and Orders. The members of a society whose values are freedom and equality behave differently, walk, speak, fight differently from the members of a slave society. Plato expressed this nastily in the Republic[17] when he said that in a democracy even the horses and asses behaved with a gait expressive of remarkable freedom and dignity, and like everyone else became 'gorged with freedom.' Suspicion, fear and servility are absent, or, at least, inconspicuous in such a society. And no one who visited Germany after 1933 needs to be reminded of the change of atmosphere.

Decisions concerning the worth of societies and social institutions are not made by an *élite,* by rulers or a governing class but, explicitly or by acceptance, by those who live and work in a society and operate its institutions. But these decisions may be changed by the effective propaganda of a minority who have reached other decisions of whose value they desire to convince the majority. Perhaps, ultimately, men get the societies and governments which they choose, even if not those which they deserve, for they may deserve better than passion, indolence or ignorance permits them to choose.

This leads to a second question. Upon what grounds or for what reasons are decisions reached? Consider the expression of the doctrine of equality; that all human beings are of equal worth, intrinsic value, or are ends in themselves. Is there an answer to the question, Why? On what *evidence* is this assertion based? How can such a decision be maintained despite the obvious differences between human beings? The answer of the natural law theorists and of Kant was that the 'natural' fact that all men have reason proves that they are of intrinsic worth, and are thus entitled to the Rights of Man. It is not clear, however, whether imbeciles and lunatics forfeit human rights. No one can deny that they are human beings. A person who becomes insane does not thereby become a mere animal. But if statements about the possession by anything of a natural characteristic is related to a decision of worth as evidence for a conclusion, then it would be illogical to retain the decision when the characteristics were absent or had changed. It is irrational to continue to believe a proposition when evidence shows that it is false. I affirm that no natural characteristic constitutes a *reason* for the assertion that all human beings are

[17] Book 8, 563.

of equal worth. Or, alternatively, that *all* the characteristics of *any* human being are equally reasons for this assertion. But this amounts to saying that the decision of equal worth is affirmed of all human beings *whatever their particular characteristics.* It does not follow that they are of equal *merit* and that their treatment should not vary accordingly, in ways compatible with their intrinsic value. But even a criminal, though he has lost merit and may deserve punishment, does not become worthless. He cannot be cast out of humanity.

I am aware that this view needs much more elaboration, and especially illustration than can be given in very limited space. I can, therefore, indicate only in a general way the type of value assertions and the manner in which they are related to each other and to other assertions. They are not related as evidence strengthening a conclusion. For decisions are not true or false and are not deduced from premises. Do we, then, decide without reason? Are decisions determined by chance or whim? Surely, it will be said, the facts have some relevance to what is decided? To say that decisions are made without reason looks like saying that we choose by tossing a coin; opening the *Works of Shakespeare* or *The Bible* at random and reading the first sentence; or shutting our eyes and sticking a pin into the list of starters to pick the Derby winner. These seem very irrational methods of choice. Nevertheless, we do sometimes choose by a not very dissimilar procedure. If two candidates for a post are of exactly equal merit, the selectors may well end by plumping for one or the other. This, it may be said, was justified because there was 'nothing to choose between them,' not that the decision bore no relation to their merits. But there are some choices into which merit hardly enters. Those involving personal relations, for instance. It would seem absurd to try to prove that our affections were not misplaced by listing the characteristics of our friends. To one who asked for such 'proof' we should reply, with Montaigne:[18]

> *If a man urge me to tell him wherefore I loved him, I feel it cannot be expressed but by answering, because it was he, because it was myself. . . . It is not one especial consideration, nor two, nor three, nor four, nor a thousand. It is I wot not what kind of quintessence of all this commixture which seized my will.*

[18] *Essays* (trans. John Florio), *Of Friendship.*

Yet it is also correct to say that our decisions about worth are not merely arbitrary, and intelligent choices are not random. They cannot be proved correct by evidence. Nor, I suggest, do we try to prove them. What we do is to support and defend our decisions. The relation of the record of a decision to the considerations which support it is not that of proof to conclusion. It is much more like the defence of his client by a good counsel.

Consider an analogous situation in art. Suppose one were trying to defend a view that Keats is a greater poet than Crabbe. One would compare passages from each writer, showing the richness and complexity of the imagery and movement of Keats's verse and the monotonous rhythm, moral platitudes and poverty-stricken images of Crabbe. One would aid the effect by reading passages aloud for their comparable musical effects; would dwell on single lines and passages which show the differences between the evocative language of Keats and the conventional 'poetic diction' of Crabbe. The 'Season of mists and mellow fruitfulness' of the one and the 'finny tribes,' etc., of the other. One might eventually resort to the remarks of the best critics on both writers. In short, one would employ every device to 'present' Keats, to build up a convincing advocacy of his poetry. And the resistance of Crabbe's defender might collapse, and he would declare the case won with the verdict 'Keats is the better poet.' But nothing would have been *proved.* Crabbe's supporter might still disagree. He would dwell on Crabbe's 'sincerity'; his genuine sympathy with the poor and excuse his poetic limitations as due to a bad tradition for which he was not responsible. He might add that Crabbe was one of Jane Austen's favourite poets. And if he so persisted he would not be *wrong,* i.e. he would not be believing falsely that Crabbe was a better poet than Keats but much more persuasion would be needed to induce him to alter his decision.

Compare with this the correct attitude to the proof of a scientific law. If the empirical evidence is conclusive then a person who rejects the conclusion is either stupid or biased. He is certainly believing a false proposition. We do not 'defend' the law of gravitation but all instructed persons accept the proof of the law.

On the other hand, we do not refer to Mill's proof but to his 'magnificent defence' of civil liberty. For a successful defence involves much more than statement of facts. The facts of the case are known to both the prosecuting and defending counsel. The question is, should the accused be condemned or acquitted? The skilful lawyer uses these facts, but he uses them differently from the scientist. He marshals them so as to emphasize those which favour his client. He interprets those which appear unfavourable in terms of legal decisions in similar cases which would benefit the accused. He chooses language which does not merely state, but impress: he uses voice, gesture, facial expression, all the devices of eloquence and style in order to influence the decision of the jury in favour of his client. His client may still lose, but he would admit that he has a better chance of winning if he briefs a good counsel.

But, it may be asked, is this a recommendation to take fraudulent advocacy as our model for defending the rights of man? Not at all. Lawyers and art critics are not frauds, but neither are they scientists. They are more like artists who use material with results which impress and convince but do not *prove*. There is no conceivable method of *proving* that Keats is a better poet than Crabbe or that freedom is better than slavery. For assertions of value cannot be subjected to demonstrative or inductive methods. It is for this reason that such assertions have been regarded as simple expressions of feeling or emotion like cries of pain and anger. But we do not defend or support a cry of pain or shout of joy though it may be related to a cause. If our value choices are defensible their defence requires other methods.

The lawyer says: 'I agree that my client was on the premises; I deny that his being there in those circumstances constitutes a *trespass*. This may be confirmed from *Gower* v. *Flint* where this ruling was given in similar circumstances.' The critic says: 'You agree that Keats's imagery is *rich* and *complex;* his language *original* and *powerful:* that Crabbe, on the contrary, is *frigid* and *conventional* in language; *meagre* in imagery, etc. etc.' The lawyer supports his plea from previous decisions. The critic likewise appeals not to physical or psychological facts about the occurrences of marks on paper, internal pictures, etc., but to previous decisions *evaluating* these and other occurrences. Rich and powerful poetry is good; frigid and meagre versifying is bad. If we stand by our previous decisions it does not follow that we *must* on account of them make a further decision now, but they are certainly relevant. Incorporated into a system of skilful advocacy they may win a favourable verdict. But, on the other hand, we may reject our former decisions. Elaborate imagery; lyrical quality, are dismissed as *barbarous* or *sentimental;* our choice is now for the *plain* and *elegant* statement. Such a complete change in systems of evaluation seems to occur in different ages. The eighteenth century listened to Shakespeare, but gave the palm to Pope. The Victorians saw Georgian houses but chose sham Gothic. So we may present the authoritarian with an attractive picture of a free and democratic society, and if he already values independence, experimentation, mutual trust, he may agree that these values are realized in such a society. But he may call independence, insolence; experimentation, rash meddling; and the picture will fail in its effect.

There are no certainties in the field of values. For there are no true or false beliefs about values, but only better or worse decisions and choices. And to encourage the better decisions we need to employ devices which are artistic rather than scientific. For our aim is not intellectual assent, but practical effects. These are not, of course, absolutely separate, for intellectual assent to a proposition or theory is followed by using it. But values, I think, concern only behaviour. They are not known, but accepted and acted upon.

Intellectuals often complain that political propaganda, e.g. is not conducted as if it were scientific argument. But if moral values are not capable of scientific proof it would be irrational to treat them as if they were. The result of a confusion of logical types is to leave the field of non-scientific persuasion and conviction to propagandists of the type of the late Dr. Goebbels.

H. L. A. Hart

Are There Any
Natural Rights?

I shall advance the thesis that if there are any moral rights at all, it follows that there is at least one natural right, the equal right of all men to be free.[1] By saying that there is this right, I mean that in the absence of certain special conditions which are consistent with the right being an equal right, any adult human being capable of choice (1) has the right to forbearance on the part of all others from the use of coercion or restraint against him save to hinder coercion or restraint and (2) is at liberty to do (i.e., is under no obligation to abstain from) any action which is not one coercing or restraining or designed to injure other persons.[2]

I have two reasons for describing the equal right of all men to be free as a *natural* right; both of them were always empha-

H. L. A. Hart, Fellow of University College, Oxford, recently resigned his Professorship of Jurisprudence at the University of Oxford in order to prepare the Bentham papers for publication. Hart is the author of *Causation in the Law* (with A. M. Honore), Oxford, 1959; *Law, Liberty and Morality*, New York, 1963; *Punishment and Responsibility*, Oxford, 1968; as well as numerous articles, on a wide range of topics, that have appeared in philosophical and legal journals. The essay by Hart was published in *The Philosophical Review*, Vol. 64 (1955). It is reprinted here with the permission of the author and the editors of *The Philosophical Review*.

[1] I was first stimulated to think along these lines by Mr. Stuart Hampshire, and I have reached by different routes a conclusion similar to his.

[2] Further explanation of the perplexing terminology of freedom is, I fear, necessary. *Coercion* includes, besides preventing a person from doing what he chooses, making his choice less eligible by threats; *restraint* includes any action designed to make the exercise of choice impossible and so includes killing or enslaving a person. But neither coercion nor restraint includes *competition*. In terms of the distinction between "having a right to" and "being at liberty to," used above and further discussed in Section I, B, all men may have, consistently with the obligation to forbear from coercion, the *liberty* to satisfy if they can such at least of their desires as are not designed to coerce or injure others, even though in fact, owing to scarcity, one man's satisfaction causes another's frustration. In conditions of extreme scarcity this distinction between competition and coercion will not be worth drawing; natural rights are only of importance "where peace is possible" (Locke). Further, freedom (the absence of coercion) can be *valueless* to those victims of unrestricted competition too poor to make use of it; so it will be pedantic to point out to them that though starving they are free. This is the truth exaggerated by the Marxists whose *identification* of poverty with lack of freedom confuses two different evils.

sized by the classical theorists of natural rights. (1) This right is one which all men have if they are capable of choice; they have it *qua* men and not only if they are members of some society or stand in some special relation to each other. (2) This right is not created or conferred by men's voluntary action; other moral rights are.[3] Of course, it is quite obvious that my thesis is not as ambitious as the traditional theories of natural rights; for although on my view all men are *equally* entitled to be free in the sense explained, no man has an absolute or unconditional right to do or not to do any particular thing or to be treated in any particular way; coercion or restraint of any action may be justified in special conditions consistently with the general principle. So my argument will not show that men have any right (save the equal right of all to be free) which is "absolute," "indefeasible," or "imprescriptible." This may for many reduce the importance of my contention, but I think that the principle that all men have an equal right to be free, meager as it may seem, is probably all that the political philosophers of the liberal tradition need have claimed to support any program of action even if they have claimed more. But my contention that there is this one natural right may appear unsatisfying in another respect; it is only the conditional assertion that *if* there are any moral rights then there must be this one natural right. Perhaps few would now deny, as some have, that there are moral rights; for the point of that denial was usually to object to some philosophical claim as to the "ontological status" of rights, and this objection is now expressed not as a denial that there are any moral rights but as a denial of some assumed logical similarity between sentences used to assert the existence of rights and other kinds of sentences. But it is still important to remember that there may be codes of conduct quite properly termed moral codes (though we can of course say they are "imperfect") which do not employ the notion of *a* right, and there is nothing contradictory or otherwise absurd in a code or morality consisting wholly of prescriptions or in a code which prescribed only what should be done for the realization of happiness or some ideal of personal perfection.[4] Human actions in such systems would be evalu-

---

[3] Save those general rights (cf. Section II, B) which are particular exemplifications of the right of all men to be free.

[4] Is the notion of a right found in either Plato or Aristotle? There seems to be no Greek word for it as distinct from "right" or "just" (δίκαιον), though expressions like τὰ ἐμὰ δίκαια are I believe fourth-century legal idioms. The natural expressions in Plato are τὸ ἑαυτοῦ (ἔχειν) or τὰ τινὶ ὀφειλόμενα, but these seem confined to property or debts. There is no place for a moral right unless the moral value of individual freedom is recognized.

ated or criticised as compliances with prescriptions or as *good* or *bad, right* or *wrong, wise* or *foolish, fitting* or *unfitting,* but no one in such a system would have, exercise, or claim rights, or violate or infringe them. So those who lived by such systems could not of course be committed to the recognition of the equal right of all to be free; nor, I think (and this is one respect in which the notion of a right differs from other moral notions), could any parallel argument be constructed to show that, from the bare fact that actions were recognized as ones which ought or ought not to be done, as right, wrong, good or bad, it followed that some specific kind of conduct fell under these categories.

I

(A) Lawyers have for their own purposes carried the dissection of the notion of a legal right some distance, and some of their results[5] are of value in the elucidation of statements of the form "X has a right to . . ." outside legal contexts. There is of course no simple identification to be made between moral and legal rights, but there is an intimate connection between the two, and this itself is one feature which distinguishes a moral right from other fundamental moral concepts. It is not merely that as a matter of fact men speak of their moral rights mainly when advocating their incorporation in a legal system, but that the concept of a right belongs to that branch of morality which is specifically concerned to determine when one person's freedom may be limited by another's[6] and so to determine what actions may appropriately be made the subject of coercive legal rules. The words *"droit," "diritto,"* and *"Recht,"* used by continental jurists, have no simple English translation and seem to English jurists to hover uncertainly between law and morals, but they do in fact mark off an area of morality (the morality of law) which has special characteristics. It is occupied by the concepts of justice, fairness, rights, and obligation (if this last is not used as it is by many moral philosophers as

[5] As W. D. Lamont has seen: cf. his *Principles of Moral Judgment* (Oxford, 1946); for the jurists, cf. Hohfeld's *Fundamental Legal Conceptions* (New Haven, 1923).

[6] Here and subsequently I use "interfere with another's freedom," "limit another's freedom," "determine how another shall act," to mean either the use of coercion or demanding that a person shall do or not do some action. The connection between these two types of "interference" is too complex for discussion here; I think it is enough for present purposes to point out that having a justification for demanding that a person shall or shall not do some action is a necessary though not a sufficient condition for justifying coercion.

an obscuring general label to cover every action that morally we ought to do or forbear from doing). The most important common characteristic of this group of moral concepts is that there is no incongruity, but a special congruity in the use of force or the threat of force to secure that what is just or fair or someone's right to have done shall in fact be done; for it is in just these circumstances that coercion of another human being is legitimate. Kant, in the *Rechtslehre,* discusses the obligations which arise in this branch of morality under the title of *officia juris,* "which do not require that respect for duty shall be of itself the determining principle of the will," and contrasts them with *officia virtutis,* which have no moral worth unless done for the sake of the moral principle. His point is, I think, that we must distinguish from the rest of morality those principles regulating the proper distribution of human freedom which alone make it morally legitimate for one human being to determine by his choice how another should act; and a certain specific moral value is secured (to be distinguished from moral virtue in which the good will is manifested) if human relationships are conducted in accordance with these principles even though coercion has to be used to secure this, for only if these principles are regarded will freedom be distributed among human beings as it should be. And it is I think a very important feature of a moral right that the possessor of it is conceived as having a moral justification for limiting the freedom of another and that he has this justification not because the action he is entitled to require of another has some moral quality but simply because in the circumstances a certain distribution of human freedom will be maintained if he by his choice is allowed to determine how that other shall act.

(B) I can best exhibit this feature of a moral right by reconsidering the question whether moral rights and "duties"[7] are correlative. The contention that they are means, presumably, that every statement of the form "X has a right to . . ." entails and is entailed by "Y has a duty (not) to . . . ," and at this stage we must not assume that the values of the name-varia-

---

[7] I write "'duties'" here because one factor obscuring the nature of a right is the philosophical use of "duty" and "obligation" for all cases where there are moral reasons for saying an action ought to be done or not done. In fact "duty," "obligation," "right," and "good" come from different segments of morality, concern different types of conduct, and make different types of moral criticism or evaluation. Most important are the points (1) that obligations may be voluntarily incurred or created, (2) that they are *owed to* special persons (who have rights), (3) that they do not arise out of the character of the actions which are obligatory but out of the relationship of the parties. Language roughly though not consistently confines the use of "having an obligation" to such cases.

bles "X" and "Y" must be different persons. Now there is certainly one sense of "a right" (which I have already mentioned) such that it does not follow from X's having a right that X or someone else has any duty. Jurists have isolated rights in this sense and have referred to them as "liberties" just to distinguish them from rights in the centrally important sense of "right" which has "duty" as a correlative. The former sense of "right" is needed to describe those areas of social life where competition is at least morally unobjectionable. Two people walking along both see a ten-dollar bill in the road twenty yards away, and there is no clue as to the owner. Neither of the two are under a "duty" to allow the other to pick it up; each has in this sense a right to pick it up. Of course there may be many things which each has a "duty" not to do in the course of the race to the spot—neither may kill or wound the other—and corresponding to these "duties" there are rights to forbearances. The moral propriety of all economic competition implies this minimum sense of "a right" in which to say that "X has a right to" means merely that X is under no "duty" not to. Hobbes saw that the expression "a right" could have this sense but he was wrong if he thought that there is no sense in which it does follow from X's having a right that Y has a duty or at any rate an obligation.

(C) More important for our purpose is the question whether for all moral "duties" there are correlative moral rights, because those who have given an affirmative answer to this question have usually assumed without adequate scrutiny that to have a right is simply to be capable of benefiting by the performance of a "duty"; whereas in fact this is not a sufficient condition (and probably not a necessary condition) of having a right. Thus animals and babies who stand to benefit by our performance of our "duty" not to ill-treat them are said *therefore* to have rights to proper treatment. The full consequence of this reasoning is not usually followed out; most have shrunk from saying that we have rights against ourselves because we stand to benefit from our performance of our "duty" to keep ourselves alive or develop our talents. But the moral situation which arises from a promise (where the legal-sounding terminology of rights and obligations is most appropriate) illustrates most clearly that the notion of having a right and that of benefiting by the performance of a "duty" are not identical. X promises Y in return for some favor that he will look after Y's aged mother in his absence. Rights arise out of this transaction, but it is surely Y to whom the promise has been made and not his mother who *has* or *possesses* these rights. Certainly Y's mother is a person concerning whom X has an obligation and a person who will benefit by its performance, but the person *to whom* he has an obligation to look after her is Y. This is something *due to* or *owed to* Y, so it is Y, not his mother, whose right X will disregard and to whom X will have done *wrong* if he fails to keep his promise, though the mother may be physically injured. And it is Y who has a moral *claim* upon X, is *entitled* to have his mother looked after, and who can *waive* the claim and *release* Y from the obligation. Y is, in other words, morally in a position to determine by his choice how X shall act and in this way to limit X's freedom of choice; and it is this fact, not the fact that he stands to benefit, that makes it appropriate to say that he has a *right.* Of course often the person to whom a promise has been made will be the only person who stands to benefit by its performance, but this does not justify the identification of "having a right" with "benefiting by the performance of a duty." It is important for the whole logic of rights that, while the person who stands to benefit by the performance of a duty is discovered by considering what will happen if the duty is not performed, the person who has a right (to whom performance is *owed* or *due*) is discovered by examining the transaction or antecedent situation or relations of the parties out of which the "duty" arises. These considerations should incline us not to extend to animals and babies whom it is wrong to ill-treat the notion of a right to proper treatment, for the moral situation can be simply and adequately described here by saying that it is wrong or that we ought not to ill-treat them or, in the philosopher's generalized sense of "duty," that we have a duty not to ill-treat them.[8] If common usage sanctions talk of the rights of animals or babies it makes an idle use of the expression "a right," which will confuse the situation with other different moral situations where the expression "a right" has a specific force and cannot be replaced by the other moral expressions which I have mentioned. Perhaps some clarity on this matter is to be gained by considering the force of the preposition "to" in the expression "having a duty to Y" or "being under an obligation to Y" (where "Y" is the name of a person); for it is significantly different from the meaning of "to" in "doing something to Y" or "doing harm to Y," where it indicates the person affected by some action. In the first pair of expressions, "to" obviously does not have this force, but indicates the person to whom the person morally

---

[8] The use here of the generalized "duty" is apt to prejudice the question whether animals and babies have rights.

bound is bound. This is an intelligible development of the figure of a bond (*vinculum juris: obligare*); the precise figure is not that of two persons bound by a chain, but of *one* person bound, the other end of the chain lying in the hands of another to use if he chooses.[9] So it appears absurd to speak of having duties or owing obligations to ourselves—of course we may have "duties" not to do harm to ourselves, but what could be meant (once the distinction between these different meanings of "to" has been grasped) by insisting that we have duties or obligations *to* ourselves not to do harm to ourselves?

(D) The essential connection between the notion of a right and the justified limitation of one person's freedom by another may be thrown into relief if we consider codes of behavior which do not purport to confer rights but only to prescribe what shall be done. Most natural law thinkers down to Hooker conceived of natural law in this way: there were natural duties compliance with which would certainly benefit man—things to be done to achieve man's natural end—but not natural rights. And there are of course many types of codes of behavior which only prescribe what is to be done, e.g., those regulating certain ceremonies. It would be absurd to regard these codes as conferring rights, but illuminating to contrast them with rules of games, which often create rights, though not, of course, moral rights. But even a code which is plainly a moral code need not establish rights; the Decalogue is perhaps the most important example. Of course, quite apart from heavenly rewards human beings stand to benefit by general obedience to the Ten Commandments: disobedience is wrong and will certainly harm individuals. But it would be a surprising interpretation of them that treated them as conferring rights. In such an interpretation obedience to the Ten Commandments would have to be conceived as due to or owed to individuals, not merely to God, and disobedience not merely as wrong but as *a wrong to* (as well as harm to) individuals. The Commandments would cease to read like penal statutes designed only to rule out certain types of behavior and would have to be thought of as rules placed at the disposal of individuals and regulating the extent to which *they* may demand certain behavior from others. Rights are typically conceived of as *possessed* or *owned by* or *belonging to* individuals, and these expressions reflect the conception of moral rules as not only prescribing conduct but as forming a kind of moral property of individuals to which they are as

---

[9] Cf. A. H. Campbell, *The Structure of Stair's Institutes* (Glasgow, 1954), p. 31.

individuals entitled; only when rules are conceived in this way can we speak of *rights* and *wrongs* as well as right and wrong actions.[10]

So far I have sought to establish that to have a right entails having a moral justification for limiting the freedom of another person and for determining how he should act; it is now important to see that the moral justification must be of a special kind if it is to constitute a right, and this will emerge most clearly from an examination of the circumstances in which rights are asserted with the typical expression "I have a right to. . . ." It is I think the case that this form of words is used in two main types of situations: (A) when the claimant has some special justification for interference with another's freedom which other persons do not have ("*I* have a right to be paid what you promised for my services"); (B) when the claimant is concerned to resist or object to some interference by another person as having no justification ("*I* have a right to say what I think").

(A) *Special rights*   When rights arise out of special transactions between individuals or out of some special relationship in which they stand to each other, both the persons who have the right and those who have the corresponding obligation are limited to the parties to the special transaction or relationship. I call such rights special rights to distinguish them from those moral rights which are thought of as rights against (i.e., as imposing obligations upon)[11] everyone, such as those that are asserted when some unjustified interference is made or threatened as in (B) above.

  (i) The most obvious cases of special rights are those that arise from promises. By promising to do or not to do something, we voluntarily incur obligations and create or confer rights on those to whom we promise; we alter the existing moral independence of the parties' freedom of choice in relation to some action and create a new moral relationship between them, so that it becomes morally legitimate for the person to whom the promise is given to determine how the

---

[10] Continental jurists distinguish between *"subjektives"* and *"objektives Recht,"* which corresponds very well to the distinction between *a* right, which an individual has, and what it is right to do.

[11] Cf. Section (B) below.

promisor shall act. The promisee has a temporary authority or sovereignty in relation to some specific matter over the other's will which we express by saying that the promisor is under an obligation *to* the promisee to do what he has promised. To some philosophers the notion that moral phenomena—rights and duties or obligations—can be brought into existence by the voluntary action of individuals has appeared utterly mysterious; but this I think has been so because they have not clearly seen how special the moral notions of a right and an obligation are, nor how peculiarly they are connected with the distribution of freedom of choice; it would indeed be mysterious if we could make actions morally good or bad by voluntary choice. The simplest case of promising illustrates two points characteristic of all special rights: (1) the right and obligation arise not because the promised action has itself any particular moral quality, but just because of the voluntary transaction between the parties; (2) the identity of the parties concerned is vital—only *this* person (the promisee) has the moral justification for determining how the promisor shall act. It is *his* right; only in relation to him is the promisor's freedom of choice diminished, so that if he chooses to release the promisor no one else can complain.

(ii) But a promise is not the only kind of transaction whereby rights are conferred. They may be *accorded* by a person consenting or authorizing another to interfere in matters which but for this consent or authorization he would be free to determine for himself. If I consent to your taking precautions for my health or happiness or authorize you to look after my interests, then you have a right which others have not, and I cannot complain of your interference if it is within the sphere of your authority. This is what is meant by a person surrendering his rights to another; and again the typical characteristics of a right are present in this situation: the person authorized has the right to interfere not because of its intrinsic character but because *these* persons have stood in *this* relationship. No one else (not similarly authorized) has any *right*[12] to interfere in theory even if the person authorized does not exercise his right.

(iii) Special rights are not only those created by the deliberate choice of the party on whom the obligation falls, as they are when they are accorded or spring from promises, and not all obligations to other persons are deliberately incurred,

---

[12] Though it may be *better* (the lesser of two evils) that he should: cf. p. 71 below.

though I think it is true of all special rights that they arise from previous voluntary actions. A third very important source of special rights and obligations which we recognize in many spheres of life is what may be termed mutuality of restrictions, and I think political obligation is intelligible only if we see what precisely this is and how it differs from the other right-creating transactions (consent, promising) to which philosophers have assimilated it. In its bare schematic outline it is this: when a number of persons conduct any joint enterprise according to rules and thus restrict their liberty, those who have submitted to these restrictions when required have a right to a similar submission from those who have benefited by their submission. The rules may provide that officials should have authority to enforce obedience and make further rules, and this will create a structure of legal rights and duties, but the moral obligation to obey the rules in such circumstances is *due to* the co-operating members of the society, and they have the correlative moral right to obedience. In social situations of this sort (of which political society is the most complex example) the obligation to obey the rules is something distinct from whatever other moral reasons there may be for obedience in terms of good consequences (e.g., the prevention of suffering); the obligation is due to the co-operating members of the society as such and not because they are human beings on whom it would be wrong to inflict suffering. The utilitarian explanation of political obligation fails to take account of this feature of the situation both in its simple version that the obligation exists because and only if the direct consequences of a particular act of disobedience are worse than obedience, and also in its more sophisticated version that the obligation exists even when this is not so, if disobedience increases the probability that the law in question or other laws will be disobeyed on other occasions when the direct consequences of obedience are better than those of disobedience.

Of course to say that there is such a moral obligation upon those who have benefited by the submission of other members of society to restrictive rules to obey these rules in their turn does not entail either that this is the only kind of moral reason for obedience or that there can be no cases where disobedience will be morally justified. There is no contradiction or other impropriety in saying "I have an obligation to do *X*, someone has a right to ask me to, but I now see I ought not to do it." It will in painful situations sometimes be the lesser of two moral evils to disregard what really are people's rights and not perform our obligations to them. This seems to me particularly obvious from the case of promises: I may promise to do something and thereby incur an obligation just because that is one way in which obligations (to be distinguished from other forms of moral reasons for acting) are created; reflection may show that it would in the circumstances be wrong to keep this promise because of the suffering it might cause, and we can express this by saying *"I ought not* to do it though *I have an obligation to him* to do it" just because the italicized expressions are not synonyms but come from different dimensions of morality. The attempt to explain this situation by saying that our real obligation here is to avoid the suffering and that there is only a prima facie obligation to keep the promise seems to me to confuse two quite different kinds of moral reason, and in practice such a terminology obscures the precise character of what is at stake when "for some greater good" we infringe people's rights or do not perform our obligations to them.

The social-contract theorists rightly fastened on the fact that the obligation to obey the law is not merely a special case of benevolence (direct or indirect), but something which arises between members of a particular political society out of their mutual relationship. Their mistake was to identify *this* right-creating situation of mutual restrictions with the paradigm case of promising; there are of course important similarities, and these are just the points which all special rights have in common, viz., that they arise out of special relationships between human beings and not out of the character of the action to be done or its effects.

(iv) There remains a type of situation which may be thought of as creating rights and obligations: where the parties have a special natural relationship, as in the case of parent and child. The parent's moral right to obedience from his child would I suppose now be thought to terminate when the child reaches the age "of discretion," but the case is worth mentioning because some political philosophies have had recourse to analogies with this case as an explanation of political obligation, and also because even this case has some of the features we have distinguished in special rights, viz., the right arises out of the special relationship of the parties (though it is in this case a natural relationship) and not out of the character of the actions to the performance of which there is a right.

(v) To be distinguished from special rights, of course, are special liberties, where, exceptionally, one person is *exempted* from obligations to which most are subject but does not thereby acquire a *right* to which there is a correlative obligation. If you catch me reading your brother's diary, you say,

"You have no right to read it." I say, "I have a right to read it—your brother said I might unless he told me not to, and he has not told me not to." Here I have been specially *licensed* by your brother who had a right to require me not to read his diary, so I am exempted from the moral obligation not to read it, but your brother is under no obligation to let me go on reading it. Cases where *rights,* not liberties, are accorded to manage or interfere with another person's affairs are those where the license is not revocable at will by the person according the right.

(B) *General rights*   In contrast with special rights, which constitute a justification peculiar to the holder of the right for interfering with another's freedom, are general rights, which are asserted defensively, when some unjustified interference is anticipated or threatened, in order to point out that the interference is unjustified. "I have the right to say what I think."[13] "I have the right to worship as I please." Such rights share two important characteristics with special rights. (1) To have them is to have a moral justification for determining how another shall act, viz., that he shall not interfere.[14] (2) The moral justification does not arise from the character of the particular action to the performance of which the claimant has a right; what justifies the claim is simply—there being no special relation between him and those who are threatening to interfere to justify that interference—that this is a particular exemplification of the equal right to be free. But there are of course striking differences between such defensive general rights and special rights. (1) General rights do not arise out of any special relationship or transaction between men. (2) They are not rights which are peculiar to those who have them but are rights which all men capable of choice have in the absence of those special conditions which give rise to special rights. (3) General rights have as correlatives obligations not to interfere to which everyone else is subject and not merely the parties to some

[13] In speech the difference between general and special rights is often marked by stressing the pronoun where a special right is claimed or where the special right is denied. "You have no right to stop him reading that book" refers to the reader's general right. "*You* have no right to stop him reading that book" denies that the person addressed has a special right to interfere though others may have.

[14] Strictly, in the assertion of a general right both the *right* to forbearance from coercion and the *liberty* to do the specified action are asserted, the first in the face of actual or threatened coercion, the second as an objection to an actual or anticipated demand that the action should not be done. The first in the face of actual or threatened coercion, the second as an objection to an actual or anticipated demand that the action should not be done. The first in the face of actual or threatened coercion, the second as an objection to such coercion; the second the absence in any one of a justification for such a demand. Here, in Hohfeld's words, the correlative is not an obligation but a "no-right."

special relationship or transaction, though of course they will often be asserted when some particular persons threaten to interfere as a moral objection to that interference. To assert a general right is to claim in relation to some particular action the equal right of all men to be free in the absence of any of those special conditions which constitute a special right to limit another's freedom; to assert a special right is to assert in relation to some particular action a right constituted by such special conditions to limit another's freedom. The assertion of general rights directly invokes the principle that all men equally have the right to be free; the assertion of a special right (as I attempt to show in Section III) invokes it indirectly.

III

It is, I hope, clear that unless it is recognized that interference with another's freedom requires a moral justification the notion of a right could have no place in morals; for to assert a right is to assert that there is such a justification. The characteristic function in moral discourse of those sentences in which the meaning of the expression "a right" is to be found—"I have a right to . . . ," "You have no right to . . . ," "What right have you to . . . ?"—is to bring to bear on interferences with another's freedom, or on claims to interfere, a type of moral evaluation or criticism specially appropriate to interference with freedom and characteristically different from the moral criticism of actions made with the use of expressions like "right," "wrong," "good," and "bad." And this is only one of many different types of moral ground for saying "You ought . . ." or "You ought not. . . ." The use of the expression "What right have you to . . . ?" shows this more clearly, perhaps, than the others; for we use it, just at the point where interference is actual or threatened, to call for the moral *title* of the person addressed to interfere; and we do this often without any suggestion at all that what he proposes to do is otherwise wrong and sometimes with the implication that the same interference on the part of another person would be unobjectionable.

But though our use in moral discourse of "a right" does presuppose the recognition that interference with another's freedom requires a moral justification, this would not itself suffice to establish, except in a sense easily trivialized, that in the recognition of moral rights there is implied the recognition that all men have a right to equal freedom; for unless there is some restriction inherent in the meaning of "a right" on the type of moral justification for interference which can constitute a right, the principle could be made wholly vacuous. It would, for example, be possible to adopt the principle and then assert that some characteristic or behavior of some human beings (that they are improvident, or atheists, or Jews, or Negroes) constitutes a moral justification for interfering with their freedom; *any* differences between men could, so far as my argument has yet gone, be treated as a moral justification for interference and so constitute a right, so that the equal right of all men to be free would be compatible with gross inequality. It may well be that the expression "moral" itself imports some restriction on what can constitute a moral justification for interference which would avoid this consequence, but I cannot myself yet show that this is so. It is, on the other hand, clear to me that the moral justification for interference which is to constitute a *right* to interfere (as distinct from merely making it morally good or desirable to interfere) is restricted to certain special conditions and that this is inherent in the meaning of "a right" (unless this is used so loosely that it could be replaced by the other moral expressions mentioned). Claims to interfere with another's freedom based on the general character of the activities interfered with (e.g., the folly or cruelty of "native" practices) or the general character of the parties ("We are Germans; they are Jews") even when well founded are not matters of moral right or obligation. Submission in such cases even where proper is not *due to* or *owed to* the individuals who interfere; it would be equally proper whoever of the same class of persons interfered. Hence other elements in our moral vocabulary suffice to describe this case, and it is confusing here to talk of rights. We saw in Section II that the types of justification for interference involved in special rights was independent of the character of the action to the performance of which there was a right but depended upon certain previous transactions and relations between individuals (such as promises, consent, authorization, submission to mutual restrictions). Two questions here suggest themselves: (1) On what intelligible principle could these bare forms of promising, consenting, submission to mutual restrictions, be either necessary or sufficient, irrespective of their content, to justify interference with another's freedom? (2) What characteristics have these types of transaction or relationship in common? The answer to both these questions is I think this: If we justify interference on such grounds as we give when we claim a moral right, we are in fact indirectly invoking as our justification the principle that all men have an equal right to be free. For we are in fact saying in the case of promises and consents or authorizations that this claim to interfere with another's freedom is justified because he has, in exercise of his equal right to be free, freely chosen to create this claim; and in the case of mutual restrictions we are in fact saying that this claim to interfere with another's freedom is justified because it is fair; and it is fair because only so will there be an equal distribution of restrictions and so of freedom among this group of men. So in the case of special rights as well as of general rights recognition of them implies the recognition of the equal right of all men to be free.

Gregory Vlastos

Justice and Equality

I

The close connection between justice and equality is manifest in both history and language. The great historic struggles for social justice have centered about some demand for equal rights: the struggle against slavery, political absolutism, economic exploitation, the disfranchisement of the lower and middle classes and the disfranchisement of women, colonialism, racial oppression. On the linguistic side let me mention a curiosity that will lead us into the thick of our problem. When Aristotle in Book V of the *Nicomachean Ethics* comes to grips with distributive justice, almost the first remark he has to make is that "justice is equality, as all men believe it to be, quite apart from any argument."[1] And well they might if they are Greeks, for their ordinary word for equality, *to ison* or *isotes,* comes closer to being the right word for "justice" than does the word *dikaiosyne,* which we usually translate as "justice."[2] Thus, when a man speaks Greek he will be likely to say "equality" and *mean* "justice." But it so happens that Aristotle, like Plato and others before him, believed firmly that a just distribution is in general an unequal one.[3] And to say this, if

Gregory Vlastos is Stuart Professor of Philosophy at Princeton University and the author of numerous articles on Greek philosophy, social philosophy, and moral philosophy. The material reprinted here, with slight change in text and notes, consists of Parts I and II of "Justice and Equality" in *Social Justice,* R. B. Brandt, ed., © 1962. Reprinted by permission of Prentice-Hall, Inc., Englewood Cliffs, New Jersey.

[1] 1131a 13.

[2] "Righteousness," the quality of acting rightly, would be closer to the sense of *dikaiosyne:* at *Nicomachean Ethics* 1129b 27ff., Aristotle finds it necessary to explain that, though his theme is *dikaiosyne,* he will not be discussing "virtue entire" or "complete virtue in its fullest sense." No one writing an essay on *justice* would find any need to offer this kind of explanation; nor would he be tempted, regardless of his theory of justice, to offer (as Plato does at *Rep.* 433ab) "performing the (social) function(s) for which one's nature is best fitted" as a *definition* of (social) "justice."

[3] Plato, *Gorgias* 508a (and E. R. Dodds *ad loc.* in Plato, *Gorgias* [Oxford, 1959]); *Rep.* 558c; *Laws* 744bc, 757a ff. Isocrates, *Areopagiticus* 21–22; *To Nicocles* 14. Aristotle, *Nic. Eth.* 1131a 15ff., and the commentary by F. Dirlmeier, *Aristoteles, Nikomachische Ethik* (Berlin, 1956), pp. 404–407.

"equal" is your word for "just," you would have to say that an "equal" distribution is an *unequal* one. A way had been found to hold this acrobatic linguistic posture by saying that in this connection *isotes* meant "geometrical equality," i.e., proportionality; hence the "equal" (just, fair) distribution to persons of unequal merit would have to be unequal. This tour de force must have provoked many an honest man at the time as much as it has enraged Professor Popper[4] in ours. We may view it more dispassionately as classical testimony to the strength of the tie between equality and justice: even those who meant to break the conceptual link could not, or would not, break the verbal one. The meritarian view of justice paid reluctant homage to the equalitarian one by using the vocabulary of equality to assert the justice of inequality.

But when the equalitarian has drawn from this what comfort he may, he still has to face the fact that the expropriation of his word "equality" could be carried through so reputably and so successfully that its remote inheritance has made it possible for us to speak now in a perfectly matter of fact way of "equitable inequalities" or "inequitable equalities." This kind of success cannot be wholly due to the tactical skill of those who carried out the original maneuver; though one may envy the virtuosity with which Plato disposes of the whole notion of democratic equality in a single sentence (or rather less, a participial clause) when he speaks of democracy as "distributing an odd sort of equality to equals and unequals alike."[5] The democrats themselves would have been intellectually defenseless against that quip. Their faith in democracy had no deep roots in any concept of human equality; the *isonomia* (equality of law) on which they prided themselves was the club-privilege of those who had had the good judgment to pick their ancestors from free Athenian stock of the required purity of blood. But even if we could imagine a precocious humanitarian in or before Plato's time, founding the rights of the citizen on the rights of man, it is not clear that even he would be proof against Plato's criticism. For what Plato would like to know is whether his equalitarian opponent really means to universalize equality: would he, would anyone, wish to say that there are no

---

[4] K. R. Popper, *The Open Society and its Enemies* (London, 1949), pp. 79–80. "Why did Plato claim that justice meant inequality if, in general usage, it meant equality? To me the only likely reply seems to be that he wanted to make propaganda for his totalitarian state by persuading the people that it was the 'just' state." He adds shortly after: "His attack on equalitarianism was not an honest attack," p. 80; and still later: "Plato's method appears to me dishonest," p. 105.

[5] *Rep.* 558c; and cf. *Laws* 757a: "For when equality is given to unequals the result is inequality, unless due measure is applied."

just inequalities? That there are no rights in respect of which men are unequal?

One would think that this would be among the first questions that would occur to equalitarians, and would have had long since a clear and firm answer. Strange as it may seem, this has not happened. The question has been largely evaded. Let me give an example: Article I of the Declaration of Rights of Man and Citizen (enacted by the Constituent Assembly of the First French Republic in 1791) reads: "Men are born and remain free and equal in rights. Social distinctions can be based only upon public utility." Bentham takes the first sentence to mean that men are equal in *all* rights.[6] One would like to think that this was a wilful misunderstanding. For it would be only too obvious to the drafters of the Declaration that those "social distinctions" of which they go on to speak would entail many inequalities of right. Thus the holder of a unique political office (say, the president of a republic) would not be equal in all rights to all other men or even to one other man: no other man would have equal right to this office, or to as high an office; and many would not have equal right to any political office, even if they had, as they would according to the republican constitution, equal right of eligibility to all offices. But if this is in the writers' minds, why don't they come out and say that men are born and remain equal in some rights, but are either not born or do not remain equal in a great many others? They act as though they were afraid to say the latter on this excessively public occasion, lest their public construe the admission of some unequal rights as out of harmony with the ringing commitment to human rights which is the keynote of the Declaration. What is this? Squeamishness? Confusion? Something of both? Or has it perhaps a sound foundation and, if so, in what? Plato's question is not answered. It is allowed to go by default.

There is here, as so often in the tradition of natural rights, a lack of definiteness which is exasperating to those who look for plain and consecutive thinking in moral philosophy. Coming back to this tradition fresh from the systems of Plato or Hobbes or Hume, with their clean, functional lines, one feels that whether or not the case for inequality has ever been proved, it has at least been made clear from both the aristocratic and the

---

[6] He assumes it entails that, e.g., "the rights of the heir of the most indigent family (are) equal to the rights of the heir of the most wealthy," the rights of the apprentice equal to those of his master, those of the madman and the idiot equal to those of the sane, and so forth. "A Critical Examination of the Declaration of Rights," in *Anarchical Fallacies*. In *Works* (London, 1843), ed. John Bowring, Vol. II, pp. 489ff., at p. 498.

utilitarian side; while the case for equality, housed in the rambling and somewhat rundown mansion of natural rights, has fared so poorly that when one puts a question like the one I just raised, one can't be sure of what the answer is, or even that there is supposed to be one. And much the same is true of several other questions that remain after one has completely cut out one earlier source of confusion: the mythological pre-history of a supposed state of nature. Taking "natural rights" to mean simply *human* rights—that is to say, rights which are human not in the trivial sense that those who have them are men, but in the challenging sense that in order to have them they need only be men—one would still like to know:

(1) What is the range of these rights? The French Declaration states: "these rights are liberty, property, security, and resistance to oppression." The imprudent beginning—"these rights are" instead of Jefferson's more cautious, "among these rights are"—makes it look as though the four natural rights named here are meant to be all the rights there are. If so, what happened to the pursuit of happiness? Is that the same as liberty? As for property, this was not a natural right before Locke,[7] and not always after him, e.g., not for Jefferson.[8] And what of welfare rights? They are not mentioned in the French document, nor are they implied by "security."

(2) Can the doctrine of natural rights find a place for each of the following well-known maxims of distributive justice:

1. *To each according to his* need.
2. *To each according to his* worth.
3. *To each according to his* merit.
4. *To each according to his* work.[9]

And we might add a fifth which does not seem to have worked its way to the same level of adage-like respectability, but has as good a claim as some of the others:

[7] Locke's argument that property is a natural right is a momentous innovation, "a landmark in the history of thought." O. Giercke, *Natural Law and the Theory of Society 1500 to 1800* (Cambridge: Cambridge Univ. Press, 1950), p. 103. But this is not to say that, if one looks hard enough, one will not find anticipations of Locke's theory. See E. S. Corwin, *The "Higher Law" Background of American Constitutional Law*, Great Seal Books edition (Ithaca: Cornell Univ. Press, 1955), p. 61, note 60; J. W. Gough, *Locke's Political Philosophy* (New York: Oxford Univ. Press, 1950, p. 80). (For some of these references, and for other useful suggestions, I am indebted to Dr. Hugo Bedau.)

[8] See, e.g., Ursula M. von Eckardt, *The Pursuit of Happiness in the Democratic Creed* (New York: Frederick A. Praeger, 1959), pp. 103–08.

[9] For a similar enumeration see Charles Perelman, *De la Justice* (Brussels, 1945).

5. *To each according to the* agreements *he has made.*

By making judicious selections from this list one can justify[10] extreme inequalities of distribution. It is thus that Plato concludes that the man who can no longer work has lost his right to live,[11] and Bentham that no just limits can be set to the terms on which labor can be bought, used, and used up.[12] Hobbes, most frugal of moral philosophers, operates with just the last of these maxims;[13] making the keeping of covenants the defining element of justice, he decimates civil liberties *more geometrico*.[14] These premises were not, of course, the only ones from which such morally dismal results were reached by these clear-headed and upright men; but they were the controlling ones. If merit or work or agreement, or any combination of the three, are made the final principles of distributive justice, it will not be hard to find plausible collateral premises from which to get such results. What then should a natural rights philosopher do with these maxims? Must he regard them as fifth-columnists? Or can he keep them as members of his working team, useful, if subordinate, principles of his equalitarian justice? Can this be done without making concessions to inequality which will divide his allegiance to equality?

(3) Finally, are natural rights "absolute," i.e., are their claims unexceptionable? If I have a natural right to a given benefit does it follow that I ought to be granted that benefit in all possible circumstances no matter how my other rights or those of others might be affected? Is this the meaning of the well-known statements that natural rights are "inalienable" and "imprescriptible"?

I believe that all these questions admit of reasonable answers which, when worked out fully, would amount to a revised theory of natural rights or, what is the same thing, a theory of

---

[10] I.e., show that such inequalities are just.

[11] *Rep.* 406e–407a.

[12] "When the question of slavery is not considered there is little to say respecting the conditions of master and its correlative conditions, constituted by the different kinds of servants. All these conditions are the effects of contract; these contracts the parties interested may arrange to suit themselves," *Principles of the Civil Code.* In *Works,* Bowring, ed., vol. 1, p. 341.

[13] The fifth: "the definition of *Injustice* is no other than *the not performance of covenant.* And whatsoever is not unjust is just." *Leviathan,* Part I, Ch. 15.

[14] That "nothing the sovereign representative can do to a subject, on what pretense soever, can properly be called injustice or injury" (*op. cit.,* Part II, Ch. 21) is presented as a logical consequence of (a) every subject is the "author" of each act of his sovereign and (b) no man can be the author of injustice or injury to himself. (a) follows from the definitions of "sovereign" and "subject," Part I, Ch. 18.

human rights: I shall use the two expressions interchangeably. Progress has been made in this direction in recent years in a number of important essays.[15] I shall borrow freely results reached by various contributors to this work, though without taking time to make explicit acknowledgments or register specific disagreements.

Let me begin with the answer to the third of the questions I raised. Are human rights absolute? All of these writers would say, "No." I am convinced that in this they are right,[16] and am even prepared to add that neither is there anything explicitly contrary to this in that branch of the classical theory which is of greatest interest to us today: in Locke, for example.[17] Locke has indeed been understood to mean that natural rights are absolute.[18] But nowhere does Locke *say* this. Contrariwise he believes many things which imply the opposite. For example, he would certainly approve of imprisonment as a punishment for crime; and we hear him recommending that beggars be detained in houses of correction or impressed in the navy.[19] Such constraints he would have to reckon justified exceptions to that freedom of movement which all persons claim in virtue of their natural right to liberty. So too he would have to think of the death penalty for convicted criminals, or of a military order which would bring death to many of those obeying it, as justified exceptions to some men's natural right to life. Even the right to property—indeed, that special form of it which is upheld more zealously than any other right in the *Second*

[15] The ones to which I am most indebted are: R. B. Perry, *Puritanism and Democracy* (New York: Vanguard Press, 1944) pp. 446ff.; Margaret Macdonald, "Natural Rights," *Proc. Aristotelian Society,* 1947–48 (reprinted in P. Laslett, *Philosophy, Politics and Society* [Oxford: Blackwell, 1956]); A. I. Melden and W. K. Frankena, "Human Rights," in *Science, Language and Human Rights* (Philadelphia, 1952); the symposium on "Are There Natural Rights?" by H. L. A. Hart, S. M. Brown, and Frankena in *Philosophical Review* 64 (1955); R. Wollheim, "Equality and Equal Rights," *Proc. Aristotelian Society,* 1955–56 (reprinted in F. A. Olafson, *Justice and Social Policy* [Englewood Cliffs, N.J.: Prentice-Hall, 1961]); R. Brandt, *Ethical Theory* (Englewood Cliffs, N.J.: Prentice-Hall, 1959) Ch. 17; A. I. Melden, *Rights and Right Conduct* (Oxford: Blackwell, 1959); and cf. H. L. A. Hart, *The Concept of Law* (New York: Oxford Univ. Press, 1961), Ch. IX, "Laws and Morals."

[16] For this I am especially indebted to discussion with Richard Brandt.

[17] Nor in the Thomist version as interpreted by J. Maritain. See his distinction between the "possession" and the "exercise" of a natural right (unexceptional and exceptionable, respectively), *Man and the State* (Chicago: Univ. of Chicago Press, 1951), pp. 101–03.

[18] E.g., E. F. Carritt, *Ethical and Political Thinking* (Oxford: Oxford Univ. Press, 1947), pp. 154ff. Brandt, *op. cit.,* p. 442. No text is cited from Locke to support this very widespread interpretation. Such statements as "the obligations of the law of nature cease not in society," *Second Treatise of Government,* 135, are too general to determine the point at issue here.

[19] See his proposals for the reform of the Poor Law submitted to the Board of Trade in 1697: H. R. Fox-Bourne, *Life of Locke* (London, 1876), vol. 2, pp. 379–81.

Treatise, one's right not to be deprived of property without consent[20]—could not be unconditional; Locke would have to concede that it should be over-ruled, e.g., in a famine when stores of hoarded food are requisitioned by public authority. We would, therefore, improve the consistency of Locke's theory if we understood him to mean that natural rights are subject to justified exceptions.[21] In any case, I shall adhere to this view here and, borrowing from current usage, shall speak of human rights as "prima facie" rights[22] to mean that the claims of any of them may be over-ruled in special circumstances.[23] Can one say this without giving away the radical difference which the traditional doctrine fixed between natural rights and all others? To this the answer would be that, though in this respect all rights are alike, the vital difference remains untouched: one need only be a man to have *prima facie* rights to life, liberty, welfare, and the like; but to be a man is not all one needs to have a *prima facie* right to the house he happens to own or the job he happens to hold. As for the "inalienability" and "imprescriptibility" of natural rights, we may understand them with this proviso to mean exactly what they say: that no man can alienate (i.e., sign away, transfer by contract)[24] a

[20] 138, 139. Cf. other references in J. W. Gough, *op. cit.,* p. 85, Note 1.

[21] Admitting that to do this is to add something of substance to his own explicit doctrine. He himself never refers to cases such as those I have mentioned as exceptions to natural rights.

[22] See Frankena, "Human Rights" (fn. 15 above), p. 127, and "Are There Natural Rights?" pp. 228ff.; Brandt, *op. cit.,* pp. 441ff. For some objections to this usage see Sir David Ross, *The Right and the Good* (Oxford: Oxford Univ. Press, 1939), p. 20; for strong opposition, Melden, *Rights and Right Conduct,* pp. 18ff. I am not entirely happy with this usage, but neither can I propose a better. Part of the objection is met by the clarification in the following note.

[23] A brief elucidation of what I understand by the terms I have used here is in order: To say that person, P, has a certain right, R, is to say that there is (i) an associated class of actions, such that any of them are *permissible* for P *and* (ii) a class of persons, *K,* and an associated class of demands, such that *if* (but not *only if*) one or more of these demands were made by P (or by someone else on P's behalf) on appropriate members of *K,* it would be *obligatory* for these persons to comply with the demand(s). (I take "obligatory"—in terms of which "permissible" is definable ["Action *A* is permissible" = Df "It is not obligatory to refrain from *A*"]—as a logically primitive notion). A "claim" is anything which could be demanded under a given right; to "assert a claim" is to make such a demand. To say that the claims of right R are "over-ruled" by those of right S in given circumstances is to say that in those circumstances the obligation to comply with demands associated with S is a stronger one (or "takes precedence over," "outweighs") than the obligation to comply with demands associated with R. (For a fuller statement of a conception of rights which has much in common with the one I am using here see e.g. David Braybrooke, *Three Tests for Democracy* (New York, Random House: 1968), Part One, Chapter 1, "The Concept of Rights Analyzed.")

[24] The normal sense of "alienate" when applied to rights in legal, or quasi-legal, contexts. To defend the inalienability (though without using this word) of one's right to be free from subjection to the arbitrary will of another, Locke thinks it sufficient to argue that one cannot forfeit this right "by compact or his own consent," *Second Treatise,* 23, and cannot "transfer to another" (135) this right by a voluntary act.

prima facie natural right, his own or anyone else's; and that no people can lose *prima facie* natural rights by prescription, e.g., in virtue of the time-hallowed possession of despotic power over them by a royal dynasty.[25]

Does this entirely allay our misgivings? It does not, and it should not. To say that a natural right is a *prima facie* right is to say that there are cases in which it is perfectly just to disallow its claim; and unless we have definite assurance as to the limits within which this may occur, we have no way of telling whether we are better off with this *prima facie* right than we would be without it. If *anything* may count as an allowable exception, then what does the right give us that we would otherwise lack? If only some things are to count, we need to know what sort of things these are to be, in order to know what, if anything, our right is worth. Richard Brandt does give us some such information. He implies that only for *moral* reasons will the exceptions be allowed.[26] This tells us something, but not enough. How can we know that moral reasons will not be forthcoming to nullify the efficacy of the natural right? From William Frankena's remarks we get something stronger: to "justicize" an exception we may adduce only considerations of justice ("just-making" ones).[27] This is better, but still not enough. What we ought to know is whether the considerations of justice which allow us to make exceptions to a natural right in special circumstances are the same considerations which require us to uphold it in general. For if we are to have two sets of "just-making" reasons, one set requiring us to uphold these rights, the other permitting us to over-rule them, we shall be in a state of moral uncertainty and anxiety about our natural rights, and our condition will not be improved if we label it with Professor Gallie "moral polyarchy."[28] We must find *reasons for our natural rights which will be the only moral reasons for just exceptions* to them in special circumstances.

---

[25] For the relevant sense of "prescription," see the *Shorter Oxford English Dictionary,* s.v., II (b): "uninterrupted use or possession from time immemorial, or for a period fixed by law as giving a title or right; hence title or right acquired by such use or possession." On prescription as the foundation of rights of government and property see, e.g., Edmund Burke: "Our constitution is a prescriptive constitution; it is a constitution whose sole authority is that it has existed time out of mind. . . . Prescription is the most solid of all titles, not only to property, but, which is to secure that property, to government," Reform of Representation in the House of Commons (1782), *Works,* Vol. 6.

[26] *Op. cit.,* pp. 410 and 446.

[27] *Supra,* p. 10ff.

[28] W. B. Gallie, "Liberal Morality and Socialist Morality," in Laslett (*op. cit.,* in n. 15 above), pp. 116ff. Each of us, in his view, is "internally divided, pulled this way and that on different issues by the claims and counter-claims of two conflicting moralities" (p. 121), each of which has its "own autonomous, i.e., not mutually corrigible, aims and standards" (p. 132).

This may look like a predictably unfulfillable demand, for it seems self-contradictory. But it is certainly not the latter. There is nothing self-contradictory about saying that reasons requiring a general pattern of action may permit, or even require, a departure from it in special circumstances. Thus my reasons for eating three meals a day are, say, pleasure and physical need; for these same reasons I might eat on special occasions four or five meals in a single day, or two or one. The analogy is not perfect, but it does give a rough idea of the lines along which we may concede justified exceptions to natural rights without jeopardizing the fundamental place they must hold in our scheme of justice, if we are to keep them there at all. And since all of them are equal rights (i.e., rights to equal treatment), a parallel observation may be made about the problem with which we started: An equalitarian concept of justice may admit just inequalities without inconsistency if, and only if, it provides grounds for equal human rights *which are also grounds for unequal rights of other sorts.* Such grounds, if we could find them, should carry right through all five of the maxims of distributive justice I listed above, showing how these maxims can be tied together as principles of justice and of the same concept of justice. I propose to identify these grounds in Section II, and then show, in Section IV, how on these grounds, supplemented by certain factual considerations, inequalities of merit may be recognized by the theory of equalitarian justice which I will expound in Section III.

II

Let me begin with the first on my list of maxims of distributive justice: "To each according to his need." Since needs are often unequal, this looks like a precept of unequal distribution. But this is wrong. It is in fact *the most perfect form of equal distribution.* To explain this let me take one of the best established rights in the natural law tradition: the right to the security of life and person. Believing that this is an equal right, what do we feel this means in cases of special need?

Suppose, for instance, New Yorker X gets a note from Murder, Inc., that looks like business. To allocate several policemen and plainclothesmen to guard him over the next few weeks at a cost a hundred times greater than the per capita cost of security services to other citizens during the same period, is surely *not* to make an exception to the equal distribution required by the equal right of all citizens to the security of their life and person; it is not done on the assumption that X has a greater right to security or a right to greater security. If the visitor from Mars drew this conclusion from the behavior of the police, he would be told that he was just mistaken. The greater allocation of community resources in X's favor, we would have to explain, is made precisely *because X's* security rights are equal to those of other people in New York. This means that X is entitled to the same level of police-made security as is maintained for other New Yorkers. Hence in these special circumstances, where his security level would drop to zero without extra support, he should be given this to bring his security level nearer the normal. I say "nearer," not "up to" the normal, because I am talking of New York as of 1961. If I were thinking of New York with an ideal municipal government, ideally supplied with police resources, I *would* say "up to the normal," because that is what equality of right would ideally mean. But as things are, perhaps the best that can be done for X without disrupting the general level of security maintained for all the other New Yorkers is to decrease his chances of being bumped off in a given week to, say, one to ten thousand, while those of ordinary citizens, with ordinary protection are, say, one to ten million—no small difference.[29] Now if New York were more affluent, it would be able to buy more equality[30] of security for its citizens (as well as more security): by getting more, and perhaps also better paid, policemen, it would be able to close the gap between security maintained for people in ordinary circumstances and that supplied in cases of special need, like that of X in his present jam. Here we stumble on something of considerable interest; that approximation to the goal of completely equal security benefits for all citizens is a function of two variables: first, and quite obviously, of the pattern of distribution of the resources; second, and less obviously, of their size. If the distributable resources are so meager that they are all used up to maintain a general level barely sufficient for ordinary needs, their reallocation to meet exceptional need will look too much like robbing Peter to pay Paul. In such conditions there is likely to be little, if any, provision for extremity of need and, what is

---

[29] These figures, needless to say, are "pulled out of a hat."

[30] This point was first suggested to me by Professor Kenneth Boulding's striking remark that "only a rich society can afford to be equalitarian," *The Economics of Peace* (Englewood Cliffs, N.J.: Prentice-Hall, 1945), p. 111. The more guarded form in which I am stating the point will protect it against apparent counter-examples to Boulding's remark, e.g., the astonishing equalitarianism that was still practiced by the Eskimos of the Coronation Gulf and the Mackenzie River early in this century (see V. Stefansson's essay in *Freedom*, Ruth N. Anshen, ed. [New York: Harcourt, Brace and World, 1940]).

more, the failure to meet the extremity will not be felt as a social injustice but as a calamity of fate. And since humanity has lived most of its life under conditions of general indigence, we can understand why it has been so slow to connect provision for special need with the notion of justice, and has so often made it a matter of charity; and why "to each according to his need" did not become popularized as a precept of justice until the first giant increase in the productive resources, and then only by men like Blanc and Marx, who projected an image of a superaffluent, machine-run society on the grid of an austerely equalitarian conception of justice.[31]

So we can see why distribution according to personal need, far from conflicting with the equality of distribution required by a human right, is so linked with its very meaning that under ideal conditions equality of right would coincide with distribution according to personal need. Our visitor misunderstood the sudden mobilization of New York policemen in favor of Mr. *X,* because he failed to understand that it is benefits to persons, not allocation of resources as such, that are meant to be made equal; for then he would have seen at once that unequal distribution of resources would be required to equalize benefits in cases of unequal need. But if he saw this he might then ask, "But why do you want this sort of equality?" My answer would have to be: Because the human worth of all persons is equal, however unequal may be their merit. To the explanation of this proposition I shall devote the balance of this Section.

By "merit" I shall refer throughout this essay to all the kinds of valuable qualities or performances in respect of which persons may be graded, provided only they are "acquired," i.e., represent what their possessor has himself made of his natural endowments and environmental opportunities.[32] The concept will not be restricted to moral actions or dispositions.[33] Thus wit, grace of manner, and technical skill count as meritorious qualities fully as much as sincerity, generosity, or courage.

---

[31] The well-known maxim, "from each according to his ability, to each according to his need" (Karl Marx, *Critique of the Gotha Programme,* 1875), echoes, without acknowledgment, a remark in the 9th edition of Louis Blanc's *L'Organization du travail* (Paris, 1850) that "true equality" is that "which apportions work to ability and recompense to needs" (cited in D. O. Wagner, *Social Reformers* [New York: The Macmillan Co., 1946], p. 248).

[32] This is only one of the senses recognized by the dictionary (*The Shorter Oxford English Dictionary,* s.v., 4 and 6): "Excellence," "An Excellence," the latter being illustrated by "Would you ask for his merits? Alas! he has none" (from Goldsmith). In the other senses listed by the dictionary the word either *means* "desert" or at least includes this in its meaning. On the present use of "merit" the connection with "desert" is synthetic.

[33] As is done by some philosophical moralists, e.g., Sir David Ross, *op. cit.,* pp. 135ff., where "merit" and (moral) "virtue" are co-extensive.

Given the immense variety of individual differences, it will be commonly the case that of any two persons either may excel the other in respect of different kinds or sub-kinds of merit. Thus if A and B are both clever and brave men, A may be much the cleverer as a business man, B as a literary critic, and A may excel in physical, B in moral, courage. It should be clear from just this that to speak of "a person's merit" will be strictly senseless except insofar as this is an elliptical way of referring to that person's merits, i.e., to those specifiable qualities or activities in which he rates well. So if there is a value attaching to the person himself as an integral and unique individual, *this* value will not fall under merit or be reducible to it. For it is of the essence of merit, as here defined, to be a grading concept; and there is no way of grading individuals as such. We can only grade them with respect to their qualities, hence only by abstracting from their individuality. If A is valued for some meritorious quality, *m,* his individuality does not enter into the valuation. As an individual he is then dispensable; his place could be taken without loss of value by any other individual with as good an *m*-rating. Nor would matters change by multiplying and diversifying the meritorious qualities with which A is endowed. No matter how enviable a package of well-rounded excellence A may represent, it would still follow that, if he is valued only for his merit, he is not being valued as an individual. To be sure individuals *may* be valued only for their merits. This happens all too commonly. A might be valued in just this way by P, the president of his company, for whom A, highly successful vice-president in charge of sales, amusing dinner-guest, and fine asset to the golf club, is simply high-grade equipment in various complexes of social machinery which P controls or patronizes. On the other hand, it is possible that, much as P prizes this conjunct of qualities (M), he values A also as an individual. A may be his son, and he may be genuinely fond of him. If so, his affection will be for A, not for his M-qualities. The latter P approves, admires, takes pride in, and the like. But his affection and good will are for A, and *not only because,* or *insofar as,* A has the M-qualities. For P may be equally fond of another son who rates well below A in P's scoring system. Moreover, P's affection for A, as distinct from his approval or admiration of him, need not fluctuate with the ups and downs in A's achievements. Perhaps A had some bad years after graduating from college, and it looked then as though his brilliant gifts would be wasted. It does not follow that P's love for A then lapsed or even ebbed. Constancy of affection in the face of variations of merit is one of the surest

tests of whether or not a parent does love a child. If he feels
fond of it only when it performs well, and turns coldly indiffer-
ent or hostile when its achievements slump, then his feeling for
the child can scarcely be called *love.* There are many relations
in which one's liking or esteem for a person are strictly conditional on his measuring up to certain standards. But convincing
evidence that the relation is of this type is no evidence that the
relation is one of parental love or any other kind of love. It does
nothing to show that one has this feeling, or any feeling, for
an *individual,* rather than for a place-holder of qualities one
likes to see instantiated by somebody or other close about
one.

Now if this concept of value attaching to a person's individual existence, over and above his merit—"individual worth,"[34]
let me call it—were applicable *only* in relations of personal
love, it would be irrelevant for the analysis of justice. To serve
our purpose its range of application must be coextensive with
that of justice. It must hold in all human relations, including (or
rather, especially in) the most impersonal of all, those to total
strangers, fellow-citizens or fellow-men. I must show that the
concept of individual worth does meet this condition.

Consider its role in our political community, taking the prescriptions of our laws for the treatment of persons as the index
to our valuations. For merit (among other reasons) persons
may be appointed or elected to public office or given employment by state agencies. For demerit they may lose licenses,
jobs, offices; they may be fined, jailed, or even put to death.
But in a large variety of law-regulated actions directed to
individuals, either by private persons or by organs of the state,
the question of merit and demerit does not arise. The "equal
protection of the laws" is due to persons not to meritorious
ones, nor to them in some degree above others.[35] So too for the
right to vote. One does not have it for being intelligent and
public-spirited, or lose it for being lazy, ignorant, or viciously
selfish. One is entitled to exercise it as long as, having regis-
tered, one manages to keep out of jail. This kind of arrange-
ment would look like whimsy or worse, like sheer immoralism,

[34] That this is *intrinsic* worth goes without saying. But I do not put this
term into my label, since I want to distinguish this kind of value as sharply
as possible from that of merit, and I include under "merit" not only extrinsi-
cally, but also intrinsically, valuable qualities.

[35] A modicum of merit by way of self-help and law-obedience is generally
presupposed. But it would be a mistake to think of the protection of the
laws as a reward for good behavior. Thus many legal protections are due
as much to those who will not look out for themselves as to those who do,
and to law-breakers as much as to law-observers.

if the only values recognized in our political community were those of merit. For obviously there is nothing compulsory about our political system; we could certainly devise, if we so wished, workable alternatives which would condition fundamental rights on certain kinds of merit. For example, we might have three categories of citizenship. The top one might be for those who meet high educational qualifications and give definite evidence of responsible civic interest, e.g., by active participation in political functions, tenure of public office, record of leadership in civic organizations and support to them, and the like. People in this A-category might have multiple votes in all elections and exclusive eligibility for the more important political offices; they might also be entitled to a higher level of protection by the police and to a variety of other privileges and immunities. At the other end there would be a C-category, disfranchised and legally underprivileged, for those who do not meet some lower educational test or have had a record of law-infraction or have been on the relief rolls for over three months. In between would be the B's with ordinary suffrage and intermediate legal status.

This "M-system" would be more complicated and cumbersome than ours. But something like it could certainly be made to work if we were enamoured of its peculiar scheme of values. Putting aside the question of efficiency, it gives us a picture of a community whose political valuations, conceived entirely in terms of merit, would never be grounded on individual worth, so that this notion would there be politically useless.[36] For us, on the other hand, it is indispensable.[37] We have to appeal to it when we try to make sense of the fact that our legal system accords to all citizens an identical status, carrying with it rights such as the M-system reserves to the B's or the A's, and some of which (like suffrage or freedom of speech) have been denied even to the nobility in some caste-systems of the past. This last comparison is worth pressing: it brings out the illuminating fact that in one fundamental respect our society is much more like a caste society (with a *unique* caste) than like the M-system. The latter has no place for a rank of dignity which descends on an individual by the purely existential circumstance (the "accident") of birth and remains his unalterably for life. To reproduce this feature of our system we would have to look not only

---

[36] Though it might have uses in the family or other relations.

[37] Even where a purely pragmatic justification is offered for democracy (e.g., Pendleton Herring, *Politics of Democracy* [New York: W. W. Norton & Co., 1940]) equality of worth must still be acknowledged, if only as a popular "myth" or "dogma."

to caste-societies, but to extremely rigid ones, since most of them make some provision for elevation in rank for rare merit or degradation for extreme demerit. In our legal system no such thing can happen: even a criminal may not be sentenced to second-class citizenship.[38] And the fact that first-class citizenship, having been made common, is no longer a mark of distinction does not trivialize the privileges it entails. It is the simple truth, not declamation, to speak of it, as I have done, as a "rank of dignity" in some ways comparable to that enjoyed by hereditary nobilities of the past. To see this one need only think of the position of groups in our society who have been cheated out of this status by the subversion of their constitutional rights. The difference in social position between Negroes and whites described in Dollard's classic[39] is not smaller than that between, say, bourgeoisie and aristocracy in the *ancien régime* of France. It might well be greater.

Consider finally the role of the same value in the moral community. Here differences of merit are so conspicuous and pervasive that we might even be tempted to *define* the moral response to a person in terms of moral approval or disapproval of his acts or disposition, i.e., in terms of the response to his moral merit. But there are many kinds of moral response for which a person's merit is as irrelevant as is that of New Yorker *X* when he appeals to the police for help. If I see someone in danger of drowning I will not need to satisfy myself about his moral character before going to his aid. I owe assistance to any man in such circumstances, not merely to good men. Nor is it only in rare and exceptional cases, as this example might suggest, that my obligations to others are independent of their moral merit. To be sincere, reliable, fair, kind, tolerant, unintrusive, modest in my relations with my fellows is not due them because they have made brilliant or even passing moral grades, but simply because they happen to be fellow-members of the moral community. It is not necessary to add, "members in good standing." The moral community is not a club from which members may be dropped for delinquency. Our morality does not provide for moral outcasts or half-castes. It does provide for punishment. But this takes place *within* the moral

---

[38] No one, I trust, will confuse second-class citizenship with extreme punishments, such as the death-penalty or a life-sentence, or, for that matter, with *any* legal punishment in a democratic society. Second-class citizens are those deprived of rights without any presumption of legal guilt.

[39] John Dollard, *Caste and Class in a Southern Town* (New Haven: Yale Univ. Press, 1937).

community and under its rules. It is for this reason that, for example, one has no right to be cruel to a cruel person. His offense against the moral law has not put him outside the law. He is still protected by its prohibition of cruelty—as much so as are kind persons. The pain inflicted on him as punishment for his offense does not close out the reserve of good will on the part of all others which is his birthright as a human being; it is a limited withdrawal from it. Capital punishment, if we believe in it, is no exception. The fact that a man has been condemned to death does not license his jailors to beat him or virtuous citizens to lynch him.

Here, then, as in the single-status political community, we acknowledge personal rights which are not proportioned to merit and could not be justified by merit. Their only justification could be the value which persons have simply because they are persons: the "infinite value" or the "sacredness" of their individuality, as it has often been called. I shall speak of it as "individual human worth"; or "human worth," for short. What these expressions stand for is also expressed by saying that men are "ends in themselves." This latter concept is Kant's. Some of the kinks in his formulation of it[40] can be straightened out by explaining it as follows: Everything other than a person can only have value *for* a person. This applies not only to physical objects, natural or manmade, which have only instrumental value, but also to those products of the human spirit which have also intrinsic, no less than extrinsic, value: an epic poem, a scientific theory, a legal system, a moral disposition. Even such things as these will have value only because they can be (a) experienced or felt to be valuable by human beings and (b) chosen by them from competing alternatives. Thus of everything without exception it will be true to say: if *x* is valuable and is not a person, then *x* will have value for some individual other than itself. Hence even a musical composition or a courageous deed, valued for their own sake, as "ends" not as means to anything else, will still fall into an entirely different category from that of the *valuers,* who do not need to be valued

---

[40] See, e.g., H. Sidgwick, *Methods of Ethics* (London, 1874), p. 363. For a parallel objection see the next note. Still another is that Kant, using the notion of *intrinsic worth* (*Würde* in contrast to *Preis*) to define *end in itself,* and hence as its sufficient condition, tends to conflate the value of *persons* as ends in themselves with that of their *moral merit.* Thus, though he says that "Respect [the attitude due to a being which is an end in itself] always applies to persons only" (*Critique of Practical Reason,* trans. L. W. Beck [New York, 1956], p. 79) he illustrates by respect for a person's "righteousness" (*l.c.*) and remarks: "Respect is a tribute we cannot refuse to pay to merit . . ." (p. 80).

as "ends" by someone else[41] in order to have value. In just this
sense persons, and only persons, are "ends in themselves."

The two factors in terms of which I have described the value
of the valuer—the capacities answering to (a) and (b) above—
may not be exhaustive. But their conjunction offers a translation of "individual human worth" whose usefulness for working
purposes will speak for itself. To (a) I might refer as "happiness," if I could use this term as Plato and Aristotle used
eudaimonia, i.e., without the exclusively hedonistic connota-
tions which have since been clamped on it. It will be less
misleading to use "well-being" or "welfare" for what I intend
here; that is, the enjoyment of value in all the forms in which it
can be experienced by human beings. To (b) I shall refer as
"freedom," bringing under this term not only conscious
choices and deliberate decisions but also those subtler modu-
lations and more spontaneous expressions of individual preference which could scarcely be called "choices" or "decisions"
without some forcing of language. So understood, a person's
well-being and freedom are aspects of his individual existence
as unique and unrepeatable as is that existence itself: If A and
B are listening to the same symphony with similar tastes and
dispositions, we may speak of their enjoying the "same" good,
or having the "same" enjoyment, and say that each has made
the "same" choice for this way of spending his time and
money. But here "same" will mean no more than "very similar"; the two enjoyments and choices, occurring in the con-
sciousness of A and B respectively, are absolutely unique. So
in translating *"A's human worth"* into "the worth of *A's* well-
being and freedom" we are certainly meeting the condition that
the former expression is to stand for whatever it is about A
which, unlike his merit, has *individual* worth.

We are also meeting another condition: that the equality of
human worth be justification, or ground, of equal human rights.
I can best bring this out by reverting to the visitor from Mars
who had asked a little earlier why we want equalization of
security benefits. Let us conjure up circumstances in which his
question would spring, not from idle curiosity, but from a
strong conviction that this, or any other, right entailing such
undiscriminating equality of benefits, would be entirely *un*reasonable. Suppose then that he hails from a strict meritarian

---

[41] Though, of course, they may be (if they are loved or respected as persons). In that case it will not be, strictly, the persons, but their welfare or
freedom, which will be the "end" of those who so love or respect them: since
only that which can be realized by action can be an end, to speak of another *person* as my end is bad logical grammar.

community, which maintains the *M*-system in its political life and analogous patterns in other associations. And to make things simpler, let us also suppose that he is shown nothing in New York or elsewhere that is out of line with our formal professions of equality, so that he imagines us purer, more strenuous, equalitarians than we happen to be. The pattern of valuation he ascribes to us then seems to him fantastically topsy-turvy. He can hardly bring himself to believe that rational human beings should want equal personal rights, legal and moral, for their "riff-raff" and their élites. Yet neither can he explain away our conduct as pure automatism, a mere fugue of social habit. "These people, or some of them," he will be saying to himself, "must have some reasons for this incredible code. What could these be?" If we volunteered an answer couched in terms of human worth, he might find it hard to understand us. Such an answer, unglossed, would convey to him no more than that we recognize something which is highly and equally valuable in all persons, but has nothing to do with their merit, and constitutes the ground of their equal rights. But this might start him hunting—snark-hunting—for some special quality named by "human worth" as honesty is named by "honesty" and kindness by "kindness," wondering all the while how it could have happened that he and all his tribe have had no inkling of it, if all of them have always had it.[42]

But now suppose that we avail ourselves of the aforesaid translation. We could then tell him: "To understand our code you should take into account how very different from yours is our own estimate of the relative worth of the welfare and freedom of different individuals. We agree with you that not all persons are capable of experiencing the same values. But there is a wide variety of cases in which persons are capable of this. Thus, to take a perfectly clear case, no matter how *A* and *B* might differ in taste and style of life, they would both crave relief from acute physical pain. In that case we would put the same value on giving this to either of them, regardless of the fact that *A* might be a talented, brilliantly successful person, *B* 'a mere nobody.' On this we would disagree sharply. You would weigh the welfare of members of the élite more highly than that of 'riff-raff,' as you call them. We would not. If *A* were a statesman, and giving him relief from pain enabled him to conclude an agreement that would benefit millions, while *B,* an unskilled laborer, was himself the sole beneficiary of the like relief, we would, of course, agree that the *instrumen-*

---

[42] Cf. Melden, *Rights and Right Conduct,* p. 80.

tal value of the two experiences would be vastly different—but not their *intrinsic* value. In all cases where human beings are capable of enjoying the same goods, we feel that the intrinsic value of their enjoyment is the same. In just this sense we hold that (1) *one man's well-being is as valuable as any other's.* And there is a parallel difference in our feeling for freedom. You value it only when exercised by good persons for good ends. We put no such strings on its value. We feel that choosing for oneself what one will do, believe, approve, say, see, read, worship, has its own intrinsic value, the same for all persons, and quite independently of the value of the things they happen to choose. Naturally, we hope that all of them will make the best possible use of their freedom of choice. But we value their exercise of that freedom, regardless of the outcome; and we value it equally for all. For us (2) *one man's freedom is as valuable as any other's."*

This sort of explanation, I submit, would put him in a position to resolve his dilemma. For just suppose that, taking this homily at face-value, he came to think of us as believing (1) and (2).[43] No matter how unreasonable he might think this of us he would feel it entirely reasonable that, since we do believe in equal *value* of human well-being and freedom, we should also believe in the *prima facie* equality of men's *right* to well-being and to freedom. He would see the former as a good reason for the latter; or, more formally, he could think of (1) and (2) respectively as the crucial premises in justification arguments whose respective conclusions would be: (3) One man's (*prima facie*) right to well-being is equal to that of any other, and (4) One man's (*prima facie*) right to freedom is equal to that of any other. Then, given (4), he could see how this would serve as the basis for a great variety of rights to specific kinds of freedom: freedom of movement, of association, of suffrage, of speech, of thought, of worship, of choice of employment, and the like. For each of these can be regarded as simply a specification of the general right to freedom, and would thus be covered by the justification of the latter. Moreover, given (3), he could see in it the basis for various welfare-rights, such as the right to education, medical care, work under decent conditions, relief in periods of unemployment, leisure, housing, etc.[44]

---

[43] I am bypassing the factual question of the extent to which (1) and (2) are generally believed.

[44] I am well aware of the incompleteness of this highly schematic account. It does not pretend to give the full argument for the justification of (3) and (4) (and see next note) or of their "specifications." Among other omissions, it fails to make allowance for the fact that the complex interrelations of these various rights would affect the justification of each.

Thus to give him (1) and (2) as justification for (3) and (4) would be to give him a basis for every one of the rights which are mentioned in the most complete of currently authoritative declarations of human rights, that passed by the Assembly of the United Nations in 1948. Hence to tell him that we believe in the equal worth of individual freedom and happiness would be to answer, in terms he can understand, his question, "What is your reason for your equalitarian code?"[45]

Nowhere in this defense of the translation of "equal human worth" into "equal worth of human well-being and freedom" have I claimed that the former can be *reduced* to the latter. I offered individual well-being and freedom simply as two things which do satisfy the conditions defined by individual human worth. Are there others? For the purposes of this essay this may be left an open question. For if there are, they would provide, at most, additional grounds for human rights. The ones I have specified are grounds enough.

---

[45] In "The Concept of Social Justice" (*Social Justice,* edited by R. B. Brandt [Englewood Cliffs, N.J.: 1962], p. 19), Frankena writes as though his own answer to the same question would be, "because 'all men are similarly capable of enjoying a good life' "; this, he says, is what "justifies the *prima facie* requirement that they be treated as equals." But that A and B are similarly capable of enjoying respectively good lives G(A) and G(B) is not a compelling reason for saying that A and B have equal right respectively to G(A) and G(B). The Brahmin who held (Sir Henry Maine, *Early History of Institutions* [New York, 1875], p. 399) that "a Brahmin was entitled to 20 times as much happiness as anyone else" need not have held that the Brahmin's *capacity* for happiness (or, for "enjoying a good life") differs in the same ratio from that of others. All he would have to deny would be the equal *value* of the happiness of Brahmins and of others. It is some such premise as this that Frankena must affirm to bring off his justification-argument. I might add that I am not objecting to listing capacity among the premises. The only reason I did not is that I was only citing the "crucial" premise, the one that would be normally decisive for the acceptance or rejection of the justificandum. A reference to capacity would also be necessary, and I would follow Frankena in conceding that "men may well be different in such a way that the best life of which one is capable simply is not as good as that of which another is capable" (p. 20), adding a like concession in the case of freedom. A's and B's *prima facie* equal rights to well-being and to freedom are in effect equal rights to that well-being and freedom of which A and B are equally capable. Thus where the capacity for freedom is severely limited (e.g., that of an idiot or anyone else in the *non compos mentis* class), the right to freedom would be correspondingly limited. (In a review [*Philosophical Review* 74 (1965), 406–409], J. R. Rawls takes me to task for stipulating that equality depends on capacity; he says that this "seems to abandon or qualify drastically the egalitarian intention of the essay." I am at a loss to understand this criticism. Is an egalitarian expected to hold that people have a right to do or to enjoy things which (by hypothesis) *they are not capable* of doing or enjoying? What would be the point of such a right? Perhaps Rawls is thinking of persons who lack certain (valuable) capacities at a given moment, but could *acquire* them, if they had the opportunity. But if so, is there one word in my essay which implies that these persons would not have the right to the opportunity to acquire these capacities?)

Richard Wasserstrom

Rights, Human Rights, and Racial Discrimination

The subject of natural, or human, rights is one that has recently come to enjoy a new-found intellectual and philosophical respectability. This has come about in part, I think, because of a change in philosophical mood—in philosophical attitudes and opinions toward topics in moral and political theory. And this change in mood has been reflected in a renewed interest in the whole subject of rights and duties. In addition, though, this renaissance has been influenced, I believe, by certain events of recent history—notably the horrors of Nazi Germany and the increasingly obvious injustices of racial discrimination in both the United States and Africa. For in each case one of the things that was or is involved is a denial of certain human rights.

This concern over the subject of natural rights, whatever the causes may be, is, however, in the nature of a reinstatement. Certainly there was, just a relatively few years ago, fairly general agreement that the doctrine of natural rights had been thoroughly and irretrievably discredited. Indeed, this was sometimes looked upon as the paradigm case of the manner in which a moral and political doctrine could be both rhetorically influential and intellectually inadequate and unacceptable. A number of objections, each deemed absolutely dispositive, had been put forward: the vagueness of almost every formulation of a set of natural rights, the failure of persons to agree upon what one's natural rights are, the ease with which almost everyone would acknowledge the desirability of overriding or disregarding any proffered natural rights in any one of a variety

Richard Wasserstrom is Professor of Philosophy and Professor of Law at the University of California, Los Angeles. He is the author of *The Judicial Decision*, Stanford, 1961, in addition to numerous articles that have appeared in philosophical and legal journals on a variety of topics in moral, social, and legal philosophy. The present essay was published in *The Journal of Philosophy*, Vol. 61, No. 20, October 29, 1964, and is reprinted here with the permission of the author and the editors of *The Journal of Philosophy*. It was an APA Symposium paper, read at the Eastern APA, December 27, 1964.

of readily familiar circumstances, the lack of any ground or argument for any doctrine of natural rights.

Typical is the following statement from J. B. Mabbott's little book, *The State and the Citizen:*[1]

> [*T*]*he niceties of the theory [of natural rights] need not detain us if we can attack it at its roots, and there it is most clearly vulnerable. Natural rights must be self-evident and they must be absolute if they are to be rights at all. For if a right is derivative from a more fundamental right, then it is not natural in the sense intended; and if a right is to be explained or defended by reference to the good of the community or of the individual concerned, then these "goods" are the ultimate values in the case, and their pursuit may obviously infringe or destroy the "rights" in question. Now the only way in which to demonstrate the absurdity of a theory which claims self-evidence for every article of its creed is to make a list of the articles. . . .*
>
> *Not only are the lists indeterminate and capricious in extent, they are also confused in content. . . . [T]here is no single "natural right" which is, in fact, regarded even by its own supporters as sacrosanct. Every one of them is constantly invaded in the public interest with universal approval* (57–58).

Mabbott's approach to the problem is instructive both as an example of the ease with which the subject has been taken up and dismissed, and more importantly, as a reminder of the fact that the theory of natural rights has not been a single coherent doctrine. Instead, it has served, and doubtless may still serve, as a quite indiscriminate collection of a number of logically independent propositions. It is, therefore, at least as necessary here as in many other situations that we achieve considerable precision in defining and describing the specific subject of inquiry.

This paper is an attempt to delineate schematically the form of one set of arguments for natural, or human rights.[2] I do this in the following fashion. First, I consider several important and distinctive features and functions of rights in general. Next, I describe and define certain characteristics of human rights and certain specific functions and attributes that they have. Then, I delineate and evaluate one kind of argument for human

[1] London: Arrow, 1958.
[2] Because the phrase 'natural rights' is so encrusted with certain special meanings, I shall often use the more neutral phrase 'human rights.' For my purposes there are no differences in meaning between the two expressions.

rights, as so described and defined. And finally, I analyze one particular case of a denial of human rights—that produced by the system of racial discrimination as it exists in the South today.

I

If there are any such things as human rights, they have certain important characteristics and functions just because rights themselves are valuable and distinctive moral "commodities." This is, I think, a point that is all too often overlooked whenever the concept of a right is treated as a largely uninteresting, derivative notion—one that can be taken into account in wholly satisfactory fashion through an explication of the concepts of duty and obligation.[3]

Now, it is not my intention to argue that there can be rights for which there are no correlative duties, nor that there can be duties for which there are no correlative rights—although I think that there are, e.g., the duty to be kind to animals or the duty to be charitable. Instead, what I want to show is that there are important differences between rights and duties, and, in particular, that rights fulfill certain functions that neither duties (even correlative duties) nor any other moral or legal concepts can fulfill.

Perhaps the most obvious thing to be said about rights is that they are constitutive of the domain of entitlements. They help to define and serve to protect those things concerning which one can make a very special kind of claim—a claim of right. To claim or to acquire anything as a matter of right is crucially different from seeking or obtaining it as through the grant of a privilege, the receipt of a favor, or the presence of a permission. To have a right to something is, typically, to be entitled to receive or possess or enjoy it now,[4] and to do so without securing the consent of another. As long as one has a right to anything, it is beyond the reach of another properly to withhold or deny it. In addition, to have a right is to be absolved from the obligation to weigh a variety of what would in other contexts be relevant considerations; it is to be entitled

---

[3] See, for example, S. I. Benn and R. S. Peters, *Social Principles and the Democratic State*, p. 89: "Right and duty are different names for the same normative relation, according to the point of view from which it is regarded."

[4] There are some rights as to which the possession of the object of the right can be claimed only at a future time, e.g., the right (founded upon a promise) to be repaid next week.

to the object of the right—at least *prima facie*—without any more ado. To have a right to anything is, in short, to have a very strong moral or legal claim upon it. It is the strongest kind of claim that there is.

Because this is so, it is apparent, as well, that the things to which one is entitled as a matter of right are not usually trivial or insignificant. The objects of rights are things that matter.

Another way to make what are perhaps some of the same points is to observe that rights provide special kinds of grounds or reasons for making moral judgments of at least two kinds. First, if a person has a right to something, he can properly cite that right as the *justification* for having acted in accordance with or in the exercise of that right. If a person has acted so as to experience his right, he has, without more ado, acted rightly—at least *prima facie.* To exercise one's right is to act in a way that gives appreciable assurance of immunity from criticism. Such immunity is far less assured when one leaves the areas of rights and goes, say, to the realm of the permitted or the nonprohibited.

And second, just as exercising or standing upon one's rights by itself needs no defense, so invading or interfering with or denying another's rights is by itself appropriate ground for serious censure and rebuke. Here there is a difference in emphasis and import between the breach or neglect of a duty and the invasion of or interference with a right. For to focus upon duties and their breaches is to concentrate necessarily upon the person who has the duty; it is to invoke criteria by which to make moral assessments of his conduct. Rights, on the other hand, call attention to the injury inflicted; to the fact that the possessor of the right was adversely affected by the action. Furthermore, the invasion of a right constitutes, as such, a special and independent injury, whereas this is not the case with less stringent claims.

Finally, just because rights are those moral commodities which delineate the areas of entitlement, they have an additional important function: that of defining the respects in which one can reasonably entertain certain kinds of expectations. To live in a society in which there are rights and in which rights are generally respected is to live in a society in which the social environment has been made appreciably more predictable and secure. It is to be able to count on receiving and enjoying objects of value. Rights have, therefore, an obvious psychological, as well as moral, dimension and significance.

If the above are some of the characteristics and characteristic functions of rights in general, what then can we say about human rights? More specifically, what is it for a right to be a human right, and what special role might human rights play?

Probably the simplest thing that might be said of a human right is that it is a right possessed by human beings. To talk about human rights would be to distinguish those rights which humans have from those which nonhuman entities, e.g., animals or corporations, might have.

It is certain that this is not what is generally meant by human rights. Rather than constituting the genus of all particular rights that humans have, human rights have almost always been deemed to be one species of these rights. If nothing else about the subject is clear, it is evident that one's particular legal rights, as well as some of one's moral rights, are not among one's human rights. If any right is a *human* right, it must, I believe, have at least four very general characteristics. First, it must be possessed by all human beings, as well as only by human beings. Second, because it is the same right that all human beings possess, it must be possessed equally by all human beings. Third, because human rights are possessed by all human beings, we can rule out as possible candidates any of those rights which one might have in virtue of occupying any particular status or relationship, such as that of parent, president, or promisee. And fourth, if there are any human rights, they have the additional characteristic of being assertable, in a manner of speaking, "against the whole world." That is to say, because they are rights that are not possessed in virtue of any contingent status or relationship, they are rights that can be claimed equally against any and every other human being.

Furthermore, to repeat, if there are any human *rights,* they also have certain characteristics as rights. Thus, if there are any human rights, these constitute the strongest of all moral claims that all men can assert. They serve to define and protect those things which all men are entitled to have and enjoy. They indicate those objects toward which and those areas within which every human being is entitled to act without securing further permission or assent. They function so as to put certain matters beyond the power of anyone else to grant or to deny. They provide every human being with a ready justification for acting in certain ways, and they provide each person with ready grounds upon which to condemn any interference or invasion. And they operate, as well, to induce well-founded confidence that the values or objects protected by them will be readily and predictably obtainable. If there are any human rights, they are powerful moral commodities.

Finally, it is, perhaps, desirable to observe that there are certain characteristics I have not ascribed to these rights. In particular, I have not said that human rights need have either of two features: absoluteness and self-evidence, which Mabbott found to be most suspect. I have not said that human rights are absolute in the sense that there are no conditions under which they can properly be overridden, although I have asserted—what is quite different—that they are absolute in the sense that they are possessed equally without any special, additional qualification by all human beings.[5]

Neither have I said (nor do I want to assert) that human rights are self-evident in any sense. Indeed, I want explicitly to deny that a special manner of knowing or a specific epistemology is needed for the development of a theory of human rights. I want to assert that there is much that can be said in defense or support of the claim that a particular right is a human right. And I want to insist, as well, that to adduce reasons for human rights is consistent with their character as human, or natural, rights. Nothing that I have said about human rights entails a contrary conclusion.

III

To ask whether there are any human, or natural rights is to post a potentially misleading question. Rights of any kind, and particularly natural rights, are not like chairs or trees. One cannot simply look and see whether they are there. There are, though, at least two senses in which rights of all kinds can be said to exist. There is first the sense in which we can ask and answer the empirical question of whether in a given society there is intellectual or conceptual acknowledgement of the fact that persons or other entities have rights at all. We can ask, that is, whether the persons in that society "have" the concept of a right (or a human right), and whether they regard that concept as meaningfully applicable to persons or other entities

---

[5] For the purposes of this paper and the points I wish here to make, I am not concerned with whether human rights are *prima facie* or absolute. I do not think that anything I say depends significantly upon this distinction. Without analyzing the notion, I will assume, though, that they are *prima facie* rights in the sense that there may be cases in which overriding a human right would be less undesirable than protecting it.

in that society. And there is, secondly, the sense in which we can ask the question, to what extent, in a society that acknowledges the existence of rights, is there general respect for, protection of, or noninterference with the exercise of those rights.[6]

These are not, though, the only two questions that can be asked. For we can also seek to establish whether any rights, and particularly human rights, ought to be both acknowledged and respected. I want now to begin to do this by considering the way in which an argument for human rights might be developed.

It is evident, I think, that almost any argument for the acknowledgment of any rights as human rights starts with the factual assertion that there are certain respects in which all persons are alike or equal. The argument moves typically from that assertion to the conclusion that there are certain human rights. What often remains unclear, however, is the precise way in which the truth of any proposition about the respects in which persons are alike advances an argument for the acknowledgment of human rights. And what must be supplied, therefore, are the plausible intermediate premises that connect the initial premise with the conclusion.

One of the most careful and complete illustrations of an argument that does indicate some of these intermediate steps is that provided by Gregory Vlastos in an article entitled, "Justice and Equality."[7] Our morality, he says, puts an equal intrinsic value on each person's well-being and freedom. In detail, the argument goes like this:

There is, Vlastos asserts, a wide variety of cases in which all persons are capable of experiencing the same values.

> *Thus, to take a perfectly clear case, no matter how A and B might differ in taste and style of life, they would both crave relief from acute physical pain. In that case we would put the same value on giving this to either of them, regardless of the fact that A might be a talented, brilliantly successful person, B "a mere nobody". . . . [I]n all cases where human beings are capable of enjoying the same goods, we feel that the intrinsic value of their enjoyment is the same. In just this sense we hold*

---

[6] This is an important distinction. Incontinence in respect to rights is a fairly common occurrence. In the South, for example, many persons might acknowledge that Negroes have certain rights while at the same time neglecting (out of timidity, cowardice, or general self-interest) to do what is necessary to permit these rights to be exercised.

[7] In Richard B. Brandt, ed., *Social Justice* (Englewood Cliffs, N.J.: Prentice-Hall, 1962), pp. 31–72.

that (1) one man's well-being is as valuable as any other's. . . . *[Similarly] we feel that choosing for oneself what one will do, believe, approve, say, read, worship, has its own intrinsic value, the same for all persons, and quite independently of the value of the things they happen to choose. Naturally we hope that all of them will make the best possible use of their freedom of choice. But we value their exercise of the freedom, regardless of the outcome; and we value it equally for all. For us (2)* one man's freedom is as valuable as any other's. . . . *[Thus], since we do believe in equal value as to human well-being and freedom, we should also believe in the* prima facie *equality of men's* right *to well-being and to freedom (51–52).*

As it is stated, I am not certain that this argument answers certain kinds of attack. In particular, there are three questions that merit further attention. First, why should anyone have a right to the enjoyment of any goods at all, and, more specifically, well-being and freedom? Second, for what reasons might we be warranted in believing that the intrinsic value of the enjoyment of such goods is the same for all persons? And third, even if someone ought to have a right to well-being and freedom and even if the intrinsic value of each person's enjoyment of these things is equal, why should all men have the equal right—and hence the human right—to secure, obtain, or enjoy these goods?

I think that the third question is the simplest of the three to answer. If anyone has a right to well-being and freedom and if the intrinsic value of any person's enjoyment of these goods is equal to that of any other's, then all men do have an equal right —and hence a human right—to secure, obtain, or enjoy these goods, just because it would be irrational to distinguish among persons as to the possession of these rights. That is to say, the principle that no person should be treated differently from any or all other persons unless there is some general and relevant reason that justifies this difference in treatment is a fundamental principle of morality, if not of rationality itself. Indeed, although I am not certain how one might argue for this, I think it could well be said that all men do have a "second-order" human right—that is, an absolute right—to expect all persons to adhere to this principle.

This principle, or this right, does not by itself establish that there are any specific human rights. But either the principle or the right does seem to establish that well-being and freedom are human rights if they are rights at all and if the intrinsic value of each person's enjoyment is the same. For, given these premises, it does appear to follow that there is no relevant and general reason to differentiate among persons as to the possession of this right.

I say "seem to" and "appear to" because this general principle of morality may not be strong enough. What has been said so far does not in any obvious fashion rule out the possibility that there is some general and relevant principle of differentiation. It only, apparently, rules out possible variations in intrinsic value as a reason for making differentiations.

The requirement of *relevance* does, I think, seem to make the argument secure. For, if *the reason* for acknowledging in a person a right to freedom and well-being is the intrinsic value of his enjoyment of these goods, then the nature of the intrinsic value of any other person's enjoyment is the only relevant reason for making exceptions or for differentiating among persons as to the possession of these rights.[8]

As to the first question, that of whether a person has a right to well-being and freedom, I am not certain what kind of answer is most satisfactory. If Vlastos is correct in asserting that these enjoyments are *values,* then that is, perhaps, answer enough. That is to say, if enjoying well-being is something *valuable*—and especially if it is intrinsically valuable—then it seems to follow that this is the kind of thing to which one ought to have a right. For if anything ought to be given the kind of protection afforded by a right, it ought surely be that which is valuable. Perhaps, too, there is nothing more that need be said other than to point out that we simply do properly value well-being and freedom.

I think that another, more general answer is also possible. Here I would revert more specifically to my earlier discussion of some of the characteristics and functions of rights. There are two points to be made. First, if we are asked, why ought anyone have a right to anything? or why not have a system in which there are not rights at all? the answer is that such a system would be a morally impoverished one. It would prevent persons from asserting those kinds of claims, it would preclude persons from having those types of expectations, and it would

---

[8] See, e.g., Bernard Williams, "The Idea of Equality," in P. Laslett and W. G. Runciman, eds., *Philosophy, Politics and Society,* II (Oxford: Basil Blackwell, 1962), pp. 111–113.

Professor Vlastos imposes a somewhat different requirement which, I think, comes to about the same thing: "An equalitarian concept of justice may admit just inequalities without inconsistency if, and only if, it provides grounds for equal human rights *which are also grounds for unequal rights of other sorts"* (Vlastos, *op. cit.,* p. 40; italics in text).

prohibit persons from making those kinds of judgments which a system of rights makes possible.

Thus, if we can answer the question of why have rights at all, we can then ask and answer the question of what things—among others—ought to be protected by *rights.* And the answer, I take it, is that one ought to be able to claim as entitlements those minimal things without which it is impossible to develop one's capabilities and to live a life as a human being. Hence, to take one thing that is a precondition of well-being, the relief from acute physical pain, this is the kind of enjoyment that ought to be protected as a right of some kind just because without such relief there is precious little that one can effectively do or become. And similarly for the opportunity to make choices, examine beliefs, and the like.

To recapitulate. The discussion so far has indicated two things: (1) the conditions under which any specific right would be a human right, and (2) some possible grounds for arguing that certain values or enjoyments ought to be regarded as matters of right. The final question that remains is whether there are any specific rights that satisfy the conditions necessary to make them human rights. Or, more specifically, whether it is plausible to believe that there are no general and relevant principles that justify making distinctions among persons in respect to their rights to well-being and freedom.

Vlastos has it that the rights to well-being and freedom do satisfy these conditions, since he asserts that we, at least, do regard each person's well-being and freedom as having equal intrinsic value. If this is correct, if each person's well-being and freedom does have *equal* intrinsic value, then there is no general and relevant principle for differentiating among persons as to these values and, hence, as to their rights to secure these values. But this does not seem wholly satisfactory. It does not give us any reason for supposing that it is plausible to ascribe equal intrinsic value to each person's well-being and freedom.

The crucial question, then, is the plausibility of ascribing equal intrinsic value to each person's well-being and freedom. There are, I think, at least three different answers that might be given.

First, it might be asserted that this ascription simply constitutes another feature of our morality. The only things that can be done are to point out that this is an assumption that we do make and to ask persons whether they would not prefer to live in a society in which such an assumption is made.

While perhaps correct and persuasive, this does not seem to me to be all that can be done. In particular, there are, I think, two further arguments that may be made.

The first is that there are cases in which all human beings *equally* are capable of enjoying the same goods, e.g., relief from acute physical pain,[9] or that they are capable of deriving equal enjoyment from the same goods. If this is true, then if anyone has a right to this enjoyment, that right is a human right just because there is no rational ground for preferring one man's enjoyment to another's. For, if all persons do have equal capacities of these sorts and if the existence of these capacities is the reason for ascribing these rights to anyone, then all persons ought to have the right to claim equality of treatment in respect to the possession and exercise of these rights.

The difficulty inherent in this argument is at the same time the strength of the next one. The difficulty is simply that it does seem extraordinarily difficult to know how one would show that all men are equally capable of enjoying any of the same goods, or even how one might attempt to gather or evaluate relevant evidence in this matter. In a real sense, interpersonal comparisons of such a thing as the ability to bear pain seems to be logically as well as empirically unobtainable. Even more unobtainable, no doubt, is a measure of the comparative enjoyments derivable from choosing for oneself.[10] These are simply enjoyments the comparative worths of which, as different persons, there is no way to assess. If this is so, then this fact gives rise to an alternative argument.

We do know, through inspection of human history as well as of our own lives, that the denial of the opportunity to experience the enjoyment of these goods makes it impossible to live either a full or a satisfying life. In a real sense, the enjoyment of these goods differentiates human from nonhuman entities. And therefore, even if we have no meaningful or reliable criteria for comparing and weighing capabilities for enjoyment or for measuring their quantity or quality, we probably know all we need to know to justify our refusal to attempt to grade the value of the enjoyment of these goods. Hence, the dual

[9] See, William, *op. cit.,* p. 112: "These respects [in which men are alike] are notably the capacity to feel pain, both from immediate physical causes and from various situations represented in perception and in thought; and the capacity to feel affection for others, and the consequences of this, connected with the frustration of this affection, loss of its objects, etc."

[10] At times, Vlastos seems to adopt this view as well as the preceding one. See, e.g., Vlastos, *op. cit.,* p. 49: "So understood a person's well-being and freedom are aspects of his individual existence as unique and unrepeatable as is that existence itself. . . ."

grounds for treating their intrinsic values as equal for all persons: either these values are equal for all persons, or, if there are differences, they are not in principle discoverable or measurable. Hence, the argument, or an argument, for the human rights to well-being and freedom.

Because the foregoing discussion has been quite general and abstract, I want finally to consider briefly one illustration of a denial of human rights and to delineate both the several ways in which such a denial can occur and some of the different consequences of that denial. My example is that of the way in which Negro persons are regarded and treated by many whites in the South.

The first thing that is obvious is that many white Southerners would or might be willing to accept all that has been said so far and yet seek to justify their attitudes and behavior toward Negroes.

They might agree, for example, that all persons do have a right to be accorded equal treatment unless there is a general and relevant principle of differentiation. They would also surely acknowledge that some persons do have rights to many different things, including most certainly well-being and freedom. But they would insist, nonetheless, that there exists a general and relevant principle of differentiation, namely, that some persons are Negroes and others are not.

Now, those who do bother to concern themselves with arguments and with the need to give reasons would not, typically, assert that the mere fact of color difference does constitute a general and relevant reason. Rather, they would argue that this color difference is correlated with certain other characteristics and attitudes that are relevant.[11] In so doing, they invariably commit certain logical and moral mistakes.

First, the purported differentiating characteristic is usually not relevant to the differentiation sought to be made; e.g., none of the characteristics that supposedly differentiate Negroes from whites has any relevance to the capacity to bear acute physical pain or to the strength of the desire to be free from it. Indeed, almost all arguments neglect the fact that the capacities to enjoy those things which are constitutive of well-being and freedom are either incommensurable among persons or alike in all persons.

Second, the invocation of these differentiating characteristics always violates the requirement of relevance in another

---

[11] See, Williams, *op. cit.,* p. 113.

sense. For, given the typical definition of a Negro (in Alabama the legal definition is any person with "a drop of Negro blood"), it is apparent that there could not—under any plausible scientific theory—be good grounds for making any differentiations between Negroes and whites.[12]

Third, and related to the above, any argument that makes distinctions as to the possession of human rights in virtue of the truth of certain empirical generalizations invariably produces some unjust denials of those rights. That is to say, even if some of the generalizations about Negroes are correct, they are correct only in the sense that the distinguishing characteristics ascribed to Negroes are possessed by some or many Negroes but not by all Negroes. Yet, before any reason for differentiating among persons as to the possession of human rights can be a relevant reason, that reason must be relevant in respect to *each person* so affected or distinguished. To argue otherwise is to neglect the fact, among other things, that human rights are personal and of at least *prima facie* equal importance to each possessor of those rights.

A different reaction or argument of white Southerners in respect to recent events in the South is bewilderment. Rather than (or in addition to) arguing for the existence of principles of differentiation, the white Southerner will say that he simply cannot understand the Negro's dissatisfaction with his lot. This is so because he, the white Southerner, has always treated his Negroes very well. With appreciable sincerity, he will assert that he has real affection for many Negroes. He would never needlessly inflict pain or suffering upon them. Indeed, he has often assumed special obligations to make certain that their lives were free from hunger, pain, and disease.

Now of course, this description of the facts is seldom accurate at all. Negroes have almost always been made to endure needless and extremely severe suffering in all too many obvious ways for all too many obviously wrong reasons. But I want to assume for my purposes the accuracy of the white Southerner's assertions. For these assertions are instructive just because they reveal some of the less obvious effects of a denial of human rights.

What is wholly missing from this description of the situation is the ability and inclination to conceptualize the Negro—any

---

[12] This is to say nothing, of course, of the speciousness of any principle of differentiation that builds upon inequalities that are themselves produced by the unequal and unjust distribution of *opportunities*.

Negro—as the possible possessor of rights of any kind, and a *fortiori* of any human rights. And this has certain especially obnoxious consequences.

In the first place, the white Southerner's moral universe illustrates both the fact that it is possible to conceive of duties without conceiving of their correlative rights and the fact that the mistakes thereby committed are not chiefly mistakes of logic and definition. The mistakes matter morally. For what this way of conceiving most denies to any Negro is the opportunity to assert claims as a matter of right. It denies him the standing to protest against the way he is treated. If the white Southerner fails to do his duty, that is simply a matter between him and his conscience.

In the second place, it requires of any Negro that *he* make out his case for the enjoyment of any goods. It reduces all of *his* claims to the level of requests, privileges, and favors. But there are simply certain things, certain goods, that nobody ought to have to request of another. There are certain things that no one else ought to have the power to decide to refuse or to grant. To observe what happens to any person who is required to adopt habits of obsequious, deferential behavior in order to minimize the likelihood of physical abuse, arbitrary treatment, or economic destitution is to see most graphically how important human rights are and what their denial can mean. To witness what happens to a person's own attitudes, aspirations, and conceptions of himself[13] when he must request or petition for the opportunity to voice an opinion, to consult with a public official, or to secure the protection of the law is to be given dramatic and convincing assurance of the moral necessity of a conception of human rights.

And there is one final point. In a real sense, a society that simply lacks any conception of human rights is less offensive than one which has such a conception but denies that some persons have these rights. This is so not just because of the inequality and unfairness involved in differentiating for the wrong reasons among persons. Rather, a society based on such denial is especially offensive because it implicitly, if not explicitly, entails that there are some persons who do not and would not desire or need or enjoy those minimal goods which all men do need and desire and enjoy. It is to read certain

---

[13] Vlastos puts what I take to be the same point this way: "Any practice which tends to so weaken and confuse the personal esteem of a group of persons—slavery, serfdom or, in our own time racial segregation—may be morally condemned on this one ground, even if there were no other for indicting it" (Vlastos, *op. cit.*, p. 71).

persons, all of whom are most certainly human beings, out of the human race. This is surely among the greatest of all moral wrongs.

I know of no better example of the magnitude of this evil than that provided by a lengthy account in a Southern newspaper about the high school band program in a certain city. The article described fully the magnificence of the program and emphasized especially the fact that it was a program in which *all high school students* in the city participated.

Negro children neither were nor could be participants in the program. The article, however, saw no need to point this out. I submit that it neglected to do so not because everyone knew the fact, but because in a real sense the writer and the newspaper do not regard Negro high school students as children—persons, human beings—at all.

What is the Negro parent who reads this article to say to his children? What are his children supposed to think? How does a Negro parent even begin to demonstrate to the world that his children are really children, too? These are burdens no civilized society ought ever to impose. These are among the burdens that an established and acknowledged system of human rights helps to eliminate.

Herbert Morris

Herbert Morris

Persons and
Punishment

*They acted and looked . . . at us, and around in our house, in
a way that had about it the feeling—at least for me—that we
were not people. In their eyesight we were just things, that was
all. [Malcolm X]*

*We have no right to treat a man like a dog. [Governor Maddox
of Georgia]*

Alfredo Traps in Durrenmatt's tale discovers that he has
brought off, all by himself, a murder involving considerable
ingenuity. The mock prosecutor in the tale demands the death
penalty "as reward for a crime that merits admiration, astonishment, and respect." Traps is deeply moved; indeed, he is
exhilarated, and the whole of his life becomes more heroic,
and, ironically, more precious. His defense attorney proceeds
to argue that Traps was not only innocent but incapable of
guilt, "a victim of the age." This defense Traps disavows with
indignation and anger. He makes claim to the murder as his
and demands the prescribed punishment—death.

The themes to be found in this macabre tale do not often find
their way into philosophical discussions of punishment. These
discussions deal with large and significant questions of
whether or not we ever have the right to punish, and if we do,
under what conditions, to what degree, and in what manner.
There is a tradition, of course, not notable for its present
vitality, that is closely linked with motifs in Durrenmatt's tale of
crime and punishment. Its adherents have urged that justice

Herbert Morris is Professor of Philosophy and Professor of Law at the
University of California, Los Angeles. He is the editor of *Freedom and Responsibility*, Stanford, 1961, and the author of a number of articles that have
appeared in philosophical and legal journals on a variety of topics in moral
philosophy, the philosophy of law, and the philosophy of mind. The present
essay was published in *The Monist*, 52, No. 4 (October 1968), pp. 475–501,
and is reprinted with the permission of the author and The Open Court Publishing Company, LaSalle, Illinois.

requires a person be punished if he is guilty. Sometimes—though rarely—these philosophers have expressed themselves in terms of the criminal's *right to be punished.* Reaction to the claim that there is such a right has been astonishment combined, perhaps, with a touch of contempt for the perversity of the suggestion. A strange right that no one would ever wish to claim! With that flourish the subject is buried and the right disposed of. In this paper the subject is resurrected.

My aim is to argue for four propositions concerning rights that will certainly strike some as not only false but preposterous: first, that we have a right to punishment; second, that this right derives from a fundamental human right to be treated as a person; third, that this fundamental right is a natural, inalienable, and absolute right; and, fourth, that the denial of this right implies the denial of all moral rights and duties. Showing the truth of one, let alone all, of these large and questionable claims, is a tall order. The attempt or, more properly speaking, the first steps in an attempt, follow.

1. When someone claims that there is a right to be free, we can easily imagine situations in which the right is infringed and easily imagine situations in which there is a point to asserting or claiming the right. With the right to be punished, matters are otherwise. The immediate reaction to the claim that there is such a right is puzzlement. And the reasons for this are apparent. People do not normally value pain and suffering. Punishment is associated with pain and suffering. When we think about punishment we naturally think of the strong desire most persons have to avoid it, to accept, for example, acquittal of a criminal charge with relief and eagerly, if convicted, to hope for pardon or probation. Adding, of course, to the paradoxical character of the claim of such a right is difficulty in imagining circumstances in which it would be denied one. When would one rightly demand punishment and meet with any threat of the claim being denied?

So our first task is to see when the claim of such a right would have a point. I want to approach this task by setting out two complex types of institutions both of which are designed to maintain some degree of social control. In the one a central concept is punishment for wrongdoing and in the other the central concepts are control of dangerous individuals and treatment of disease.

Let us first turn attention to the institutions in which punishment is involved. The institutions I describe will resemble those we ordinarily think of as institutions of punishment; they will have, however, additional features we associate with a system of just punishment.

Let us suppose that men are constituted roughly as they now are, with a rough equivalence in strength and abilities, a capacity to be injured by each other and to make judgments that such injury is undesirable, a limited strength of will, and a capacity to reason and to conform conduct to rules. Applying to the conduct of these men are a group of rules, ones I shall label 'primary,' which closely resemble the core rules of our criminal law, rules that prohibit violence and deception and compliance with which provides benefits for all persons. These benefits consist in noninterference by others with what each person values, such matters as continuance of life and bodily security. The rules define a sphere for each person, then, which is immune from interference by others. Making possible this mutual benefit is the assumption by individuals of a burden. The burden consists in the exercise of self-restraint by individuals over inclinations that would, if satisfied, directly interfere or create a substantial risk of interference with others in proscribed ways. If a person fails to exercise self-restraint even though he might have and gives in to such inclinations, he renounces a burden which others have voluntarily assumed and thus gains an advantage which others, who have restrained themselves, do not possess. This system then, is one in which the rules establish a mutuality of benefit and burden and in which the benefits of noninterference are conditional upon the assumption of burdens.

Connecting punishment with the violation of these primary rules, and making public the provision for punishment, is both reasonable and just. First, it is only reasonable that those who voluntarily comply with the rules be provided some assurance that they will not be assuming burdens which others are unprepared to assume. Their disposition to comply voluntarily will diminish as they learn that others are with impunity renouncing burdens they are assuming. Second, fairness dictates that a system in which benefits and burdens are equally distributed have a mechanism designed to prevent a maldistribution in the benefits and burdens. Thus, sanctions are attached to noncompliance with the primary rules so as to induce compliance with the primary rules among those who may be disinclined to obey. In this way the likelihood of an unfair distribution is diminished.

Third, it is just to punish those who have violated the rules and caused the unfair distribution of benefits and burdens. A person who violates the rules has something others have—the benefits of the system—but by renouncing what others have assumed, the burdens of self-restraint, he has acquired an unfair advantage. Matters are not even until this advantage is in some way erased. Another way of putting it is that he owes something to others, for he has something that does not right-fully belong to him. Justice—that is punishing such individuals —restores the equilibrium of benefits and burdens by taking from the individual what he owes, that is, exacting the debt. It is important to see that the equilibrium may be restored in another way. Forgiveness—with its legal analogue of a pardon —while not the righting of an unfair distribution by making one pay his debt is, nevertheless, a restoring of the equilibrium by forgiving the debt. Forgiveness may be viewed, at least in some types of cases, as a gift after the fact, erasing a debt, which had the gift been given before the fact, would not have created a debt. But the practice of pardoning has to proceed sensi-tively, for it may endanger in a way the practice of justice does not, the maintenance of an equilibrium of benefits and burdens. If all are indiscriminately pardoned less incentive is provided individuals to restrain their inclinations, thus increasing the incidence of persons taking what they do not deserve.

There are also in this system we are considering a variety of operative principles compliance with which provides some guarantee that the system of punishment does not itself pro-mote an unfair distribution of benefits and burdens. For one thing, provision is made for a variety of defenses, each one of which can be said to have as its object diminishing the chances of forcibly depriving a person of benefits others have if that person has not derived an unfair advantage. A person has not derived an unfair advantage if he could not have restrained himself or if it is unreasonable to expect him to behave otherwise than he did. Sometimes the rules preclude punishment of classes of persons such as children. Sometimes they provide a defense if on a particular occasion a person lacked the capacity to conform his conduct to the rules. Thus, someone who in an epileptic seizure strikes another is ex-cused. Punishment in these cases would be punishment of the innocent, punishment of those who do not voluntarily renounce a burden others have assumed. Punishment in such cases, then, would not equalize but rather cause an unfair distribution in benefits and burdens.

Along with principles providing defenses there are require-ments that the rules be prospective and relatively clear so that persons have a fair opportunity to comply with the rules. There are, also, rules governing, among other matters, the burden of proof, who shall bear it and what it shall be, the prohibition on double jeopardy, and the privilege against self-incrimination. Justice requires conviction of the guilty, and requires their punishment, but in setting out to fulfill the demands of justice we may, of course, because we are not omniscient, cause injustice by convicting and punishing the innocent. The resolution arrived at in the system I am describing consists in weighing as the greater evil the punishment of the innocent. The primary function of the system of rules was to provide individuals with a sphere of interest immune from interference. Given this goal, it is determined to be a greater evil for society to interfere unjustifiably with an individual by depriving him of good than for the society to fail to punish those that have unjustifiably interfered.

Finally, because the primary rules are designed to benefit all and because the punishments prescribed for their violation are publicized and the defenses respected, there is some plausibility in the exaggerated claim that in choosing to do an act violative of the rules an individual has chosen to be punished. This way of putting matters brings to our attention the extent to which, when the system is as I have described it, the criminal "has brought the punishment upon himself" in contrast to those cases where it would be misleading to say "he has brought it upon himself," cases, for example, where one does not know the rules or is punished in the absence of fault.

To summarize, then: first, there is a group of rules guiding the behavior of individuals in the community which establish spheres of interest immune from interference by others; second, provision is made for what is generally regarded as a deprivation of some thing of value if the rules are violated; third, the deprivations visited upon any person are justified by that person's having violated the rules; fourth, the deprivation, in this just system of punishment, is linked to rules that fairly distribute benefits and burdens and to procedures that strike some balance between not punishing the guilty and punishing the innocent, a class defined as those who have not voluntarily done acts violative of the law, in which it is evident that the evil of punishing the innocent is regarded as greater than the nonpunishment of the guilty.

At the core of many actual legal systems one finds, of course, rules and procedures of the kind I have sketched. It is obvious, though, that any ongoing legal system differs in significant respects from what I have presented here, containing 'pockets of injustice.'

I want now to sketch an extreme version of a set of institutions of a fundamentally different kind, institutions proceeding on a conception of man which appears to be basically at odds with that operative within a system of punishment.

Rules are promulgated in this system that prohibit certain types of injuries and harms.

In this world we are now to imagine when an individual harms another his conduct is to be regarded as a symptom of some pathological condition in the way a running nose is a symptom of a cold. Actions diverging from some conception of the normal are viewed as manifestations of a disease in the way in which we might today regard the arm and leg movements of an epileptic during a seizure. Actions conforming to what is normal are assimilated to the normal and healthy functioning of bodily organs. What a person does, then, is assimilated, on this conception, to what we believe today, or at least most of us believe today, a person undergoes. We draw a distinction between the operation of the kidney and raising an arm on request. This distinction between mere events or happenings and human actions is erased in our imagined system.[1]

There is, however, bound to be something strange in this erasing of a recognized distinction, for, as with metaphysical suggestions generally, and I take this to be one, the distinction may be reintroduced but given a different description, for

---

[1] "When a man is suffering from an infectious disease, he is a danger to the community, and it is necessary to restrict his liberty of movement. But no one associates any idea of guilt with such a situation. On the contrary, he is an object of commiseration to his friends. Such steps as science recommends are taken to cure him of his disease, and he submits as a rule without reluctance to the curtailment of liberty involved meanwhile. The same method in spirit ought to be shown in the treatment of what is called 'crime.' "
Bertrand Russell, *Roads to Freedom* (London: George Allen and Unwin Ltd., 1918), p. 135.
"We do not hold people responsible for their reflexes—for example, for coughing in church. We hold them responsible for their operant behavior— for example, for whispering in church or remaining in church while coughing. But there are variables which are responsible for whispering as well as coughing, and these may be just as inexorable. When we recognize this, we are likely to drop the notion of responsibility altogether and with it the doctrine of free will as an inner causal agent."
B. F. Skinner, *Science and Human Behavior* (1953), pp. 115–6.
"Basically, criminality is but a symptom of insanity, using the term in its widest generic sense to express unacceptable social behavior based on unconscious motivation flowing from a disturbed instinctive and emotional life, whether this appears in frank psychoses, or in less obvious form in neuroses and unrecognized psychoses. . . . If criminals are products of early environmental influences in the same sense that psychotics and neurotics are, then it should be possible to reach them psychotherapeutically."
Benjamin Karpman, "Criminal Psychodynamics," *Journal of Criminal Law and Criminology,* 47 (1956), p. 9.
"We, the agents of society, must move to end the game of tit-for-tat and blow-for-blow in which the offender has foolishly and futilely engaged himself and us. We are not driven, as he is, to wild and impulsive actions. With knowledge comes power, and with power there is no need for the frightened vengeance of the old penology. In its place should go a quiet, dignified, therapeutic program for the rehabilitation of the disorganized one, if possible, the protection of society during the treatment period, and his guided return to useful citizenship, as soon as this can be effected."
Karl Menninger, "Therapy, Not Punishment," *Harper's Magazine* (August 1959), pp. 63–64.

example, 'happenings with X type of causes' and 'happenings with Y type of causes.' Responses of different kinds, today legitimated by our distinction between happenings and actions may be legitimated by this new manner of description. And so there may be isomorphism between a system recognizing the distinction and one erasing it. Still, when this distinction is erased certain tendencies of thought and responses might naturally arise that would tend to affect unfavorably values respected by a system of punishment.

Let us elaborate on this assimilation of conduct of a certain kind to symptoms of a disease. First, there is something abnormal in both the case of conduct, such as killing another, and a symptom of a disease such as an irregular heart beat. Second, there are causes for this abnormality in action such that once we know of them we can explain the abnormality as we now can explain the symptoms of many physical diseases. The abnormality is looked upon as a happening with a causal explanation rather than an action for which there were reasons. Third, the causes that account for the abnormality interfere with the normal functioning of the body, or, in the case of killing with what is regarded as a normal functioning of an individual. Fourth, the abnormality is in some way a part of the individual, necessarily involving his body. A well going dry might satisfy our three foregoing conditions of disease symptoms, but it is hardly a disease or the symptom of one. Finally, and most obscure, the abnormality arises in some way from within the individual. If Jones is hit with a mallet by Smith, Jones may reel about and fall on James who may be injured. But this abnormal conduct of Jones is not regarded as a symptom of disease. Smith, not Jones, is suffering from some pathological condition.

With this view of man the institutions of social control respond, not with punishment, but with either preventive detention, in case of 'carriers,' or therapy in the case of those manifesting pathological symptoms. The logic of sickness implies the logic of therapy. And therapy and punishment differ widely in their implications. In bringing out some of these differences I want again to draw attention to the important fact that while the distinctions we now draw are erased in the therapy world, they may, in fact, be reintroduced but under different descriptions. To the extent they are, we really have a punishment system combined with a therapy system. I am concerned now, however, with what the implications would be were the world indeed one of therapy and not a disguised world of punishment and therapy, for I want to suggest tendencies of thought that arise when one is immersed in the ideology of disease and therapy.

First, punishment is the imposition upon a person who is believed to be at fault of something commonly believed to be a deprivation where that deprivation is justified by the person's guilty behavior. It is associated with resentment, for the guilty are those who have done what they had no right to do by failing to exercise restraint when they might have and where others have. Therapy is not a response to a person who is at fault. We respond to an individual, not because of what he has done, but because of some condition from which he is suffering. If he is no longer suffering from the condition, treatment no longer has a point. Punishment, then, focuses on the past; therapy on the present. Therapy is normally associated with compassion for what one undergoes, not resentment for what one has illegitimately done.

Second, with therapy, unlike punishment, we do not seek to deprive the person of something acknowledged as a good, but seek rather to help and to benefit the individual who is suffering by ministering to his illness in the hope that the person can be cured. The good we attempt to do is not a reward for desert. The individual suffering has not merited by his disease the good we seek to bestow upon him but has, because he is a creature that has the capacity to feel pain, a claim upon our sympathies and help.

Third, we saw with punishment that its justification was related to maintaining and restoring a fair distribution of benefits and burdens. Infliction of the prescribed punishment carries the implication, then, that one has 'paid one's debt' to society, for the punishment is the taking from the person of something commonly recognized as valuable. It is this conception of 'a debt owed' that may permit, as I suggested earlier, under certain conditions, the nonpunishment of the guilty, for operative within a system of punishment may be a concept analogous to forgiveness, namely pardoning. Who it is that we may pardon and under what conditions—contrition with its elements of self-punishment no doubt plays a role—I shall not go into though it is clearly a matter of the greatest practical and theoretical interest. What is clear is that the conceptions of 'paying a debt' or 'having a debt forgiven' or pardoning have no place in a system of therapy.

Fourth, with punishment there is an attempt at some equivalence between the advantage gained by the wrongdoer—partly based upon the seriousness of the interest invaded, partly on the state of mind with which the wrongful act was performed

—and the punishment meted out. Thus, we can understand a prohibition on 'cruel and unusual punishments' so that disproportionate pain and suffering are avoided. With therapy attempts at proportionality make no sense. It is perfectly plausible giving someone who kills a pill and treating for a lifetime within an institution one who has broken a dish and manifested accident proneness. We have the concept of 'painful treatment.' We do not have the concept of 'cruel treatment.' Because treatment is regarded as a benefit, though it may involve pain, it is natural that less restraint is exercised in bestowing it, than in inflicting punishment. Further, protests with respect to treatment are likely to be assimilated to the complaints of one whose leg must be amputated in order for him to live, and, thus, largely disregarded. To be sure, there is operative in the therapy world some conception of the "cure being worse than the disease," but if the disease is manifested in conduct harmful to others, and if being a normal operating human being is valued highly, there will naturally be considerable pressure to find the cure acceptable.

Fifth, the rules in our system of punishment governing conduct of individuals were rules violation of which involved either direct interference with others or the creation of a substantial risk of such interference. One could imagine adding to this system of primary rules other rules proscribing preparation to do acts violative of the primary rules and even rules proscribing thoughts. Objection to such suggestions would have many sources but a principal one would consist in its involving the infliction of punishment on too great a number of persons who would not, because of a change of mind, have violated the primary rules. Though we are interested in diminishing violations of the primary rules, we are not prepared to punish too many individuals who would never have violated the rules in order to achieve this aim. In a system motivated solely by a preventive and curative ideology there would be less reason to wait until symptoms manifest themselves in socially harmful conduct. It is understandable that we should wish at the earliest possible stage to arrest the development of the disease. In the punishment system, because we are dealing with deprivations, it is understandable that we should forbear from imposing them until we are quite sure of guilt. In the therapy system, dealing as it does with benefits, there is less reason for forbearance from treatment at an early stage.

Sixth, a variety of procedural safeguards we associate with punishment have less significance in a therapy system. To the degree objections to double jeopardy and self-incrimination are based on a wish to decrease the chances of the innocent being convicted and punished, a therapy system, unconcerned with this problem, would disregard such safeguards. When one is out to help people there is also little sense in urging that the burden of proof be on those providing the help. And there is less point to imposing the burden of proving that the conduct was pathological beyond a reasonable doubt. Further, a jury system which, within a system of justice, serves to make accommodations to the individual situation and to introduce a human element, would play no role or a minor one in a world where expertise is required in making determinations of disease and treatment.

In our system of punishment an attempt was made to maximize each individual's freedom of choice by first of all delimiting by rules certain spheres of conduct immune from interference by others. The punishment associated with these primary rules paid deference to an individual's free choice by connecting punishment to a freely chosen act violative of the rules, thus giving some plausibility to the claim, as we saw, that what a person received by way of punishment he himself had chosen. With the world of disease and therapy all this changes and the individual's free choice ceases to be a determinative factor in how others respond to him. All those principles of our own legal system that minimize the chances of punishment of those who have not chosen to do acts violative of the rules tend to lose their point in the therapy system, for how we respond in a therapy system to a person is not conditioned upon what he has chosen but rather on what symptoms he has manifested or may manifest and what the best therapy for the disease is that is suggested by the symptoms.

Now, it is clear I think, that were we confronted with the alternatives I have sketched, between a system of just punishment and a thoroughgoing system of treatment, a system, that is, that did not reintroduce concepts appropriate to punishment, we could see the point in claiming that a person has a right to be punished, meaning by this that a person had a right to all those institutions and practices linked to punishment. For these would provide him with, among other things, a far greater ability to predict what would happen to him on the occurrence of certain events than the therapy system. There is the inestimable value to each of us of having the responses of others to us determined over a wide range of our lives by what we choose rather than what they choose. A person has a right to institutions that respect his choices. Our punishment system does; our therapy system does not.

Apart from those aspects of our therapy model which would relate to serious limitations on personal liberty, there are clearly objections of a more profound kind to the mode of thinking I have associated with the therapy model.

First, human beings pride themselves in having capacities that animals do not. A common way, for example, of arousing shame in a child is to compare the child's conduct to that of an animal. In a system where all actions are assimilated to happenings we are assimilated to creatures—indeed, it is more extreme than this—whom we have always thought possessed of less than we. Fundamental to our practice of praise and order of attainment is that one who can do more—one who is capable of more and one who does more is more worthy of respect and admiration. And we have thought of ourselves as capable where animals are not of making, of creating, among other things, ourselves. The conception of man I have outlined would provide us with a status that today, when our conduct is assimilated to it in moral criticism, we consider properly evocative of shame.

Second, if all human conduct is viewed as something men undergo, thrown into question would be the appropriateness of that extensive range of peculiarly human satisfactions that derive from a sense of achievement. For these satisfactions we shall have to substitute those mild satisfactions attendant upon a healthy well-functioning body. Contentment is our lot if we are fortunate; intense satisfaction at achievement is entirely inappropriate.

Third, in the therapy world nothing is earned and what we receive comes to us through compassion, or through a desire to control us. Resentment is out of place. We can take credit for nothing but must always regard ourselves—if there are selves left to regard once actions disappear—as fortunate recipients of benefits or unfortunate carriers of disease who must be controlled. We know that within our own world human beings who have been so regarded and who come to accept this view of themselves come to look upon themselves as worthless. When what we do is met with resentment, we are indirectly paid something of a compliment.

Fourth, attention should also be drawn to a peculiar evil that may be attendant upon regarding a man's actions as symptoms of disease. The logic of cure will push us toward forms of therapy that inevitably involve changes in the person made against his will. The evil in this would be most apparent in those cases where the agent, whose action is determined to be a manifestation of some disease, does not regard his action in this way. He believes that what he has done is, in fact, 'right' but his conception of 'normality' is not the therapeutically accepted one. When we treat an illness we normally treat a condition that the person is not responsible for. He is 'suffering' from some disease and we treat the condition, relieving the person of something preventing his normal functioning. When we begin treating persons for actions that have been chosen, we do not lift from the person something that is interfering with his normal functioning but we change the person so that he functions in a way regarded as normal by the current therapeutic community. We have to change him and his judgments of value. In doing this we display a lack of respect for the moral status of individuals, that is, a lack of respect for the reasoning and choices of individuals. They are but animals who must be conditioned. I think we can understand and, indeed, sympathize with a man's preferring death to being forcibly turned into what he is not.

Finally, perhaps most frightening of all would be the derogation in status of all protests to treatment. If someone believes that he has done something right, and if he protests being treated and changed, the protest will itself be regarded as a sign of some pathological condition, for who would not wish to be cured of an affliction? What this leads to are questions of an important kind about the effect of this conception of man upon what we now understand by reasoning. Here what a person takes to be a reasoned defense of an act is treated, as the action was, on the model of a happening of a pathological kind. Not just a person's acts are taken from him but also his attempt at a reasoned justification for the acts. In a system of punishment a person who has committed a crime may argue that what he did was right. We make him pay the price and we respect his right to retain the judgment he has made. A conception of pathology precludes this form of respect.

It might be objected to the foregoing that all I have shown—if that—is that if the only alternatives open to us are a *just* system of punishment or the mad world of being treated like sick or healthy animals, we do in fact have a right to a system of punishment of this kind. But this hardly shows that we have a right *simpliciter* to punishment as we do, say, to be free. Indeed, it does not even show a right to a just system of punishment, for surely we can, without too much difficulty, imagine situations in which the alternatives to punishment are not this mad world but a world in which we are still treated as persons and there is, for example, not the pain and suffering attendant upon punishment. One such world is one in which there are rules but responses to their violation is not the deprivation of some good but forgiveness. Still another type of world would be one in which violation of the rules were responded to by merely comparing the conduct of the person to something commonly regarded as low or filthy, and thus, producing by this mode of moral criticism, feelings of shame rather than feelings of guilt.

I am prepared to allow that these objections have a point. While granting force to the above objections I want to offer a few additional comments with respect to each of them. First, any existent legal system permits the punishment of individuals under circumstances where the conditions I have set forth for a just system have not been satisfied. A glaring example of this would be criminal strict liability which is to be found in our own legal system. Nevertheless, I think it would be difficult to present any system we should regard as a system of punishment that would not still have a great advantage over our imagined therapy system. The system of punishment we imagine may more and more approximate a system of sheer terror in which human beings are treated as animals to be intimidated and prodded. To the degree that the system is of this character it is, in my judgment, not simply an unjust system but one that diverges from what we normally understand by a system of punishment. At least some deference to the choice of individuals is built into the idea of punishment. So there would be some truth in saying we have a right to any system of punishment if the only alternative to it was therapy.

Second, people may imagine systems in which there are rules and in which the response to their violation is not punishment but pardoning, the legal analogue of forgiveness. Surely this is a system to which we would claim a right as against one in which we are made to suffer for violating the rules. There are several comments that need to be made about this. It may be, of course, that a high incidence of pardoning would increase the incidence of rule violations. Further, the difficulty with suggesting pardoning as a general response is that pardoning presupposes the very responses that it is suggested it supplant. A system of deprivations, or a practice of deprivations on the happening of certain actions, underlies the practice of pardoning and forgiving, for it is only where we possess the idea of a wrong to be made up or of a debt owed to others, ideas we acquire within a world in which there have been deprivations for wrong acts, that we have the idea of pardoning for the wrong or forgiving the debt.

Finally, if we look at the responses I suggested would give

rise to feelings of shame, we may rightly be troubled with the appropriateness of this response in any community in which each person assumes burdens so that each may derive benefits. In such situations might it not be that individuals have a right to a system of punishment so that each person could be assured that inequities in the distribution of benefits and burdens are unlikely to occur and if they do, procedures exist for correcting them? Further, it may well be that, everything considered, we should prefer the pain and suffering of a system of punishment to a world in which we only experience shame on the doing of wrong acts, for with guilt there are relatively simple ways of ridding ourselves of the feeling we have, that is, gaining forgiveness or taking the punishment, but with shame we have to bear it until we no longer are the person who has behaved in the shameful way. Thus, I suggest that we have, wherever there is a distribution of benefits and burdens of the kind I have described, a right to a system of punishment.

I want also to make clear in concluding this section that I have argued, though very indirectly, not just for a right to a system of punishment, but for a right to be punished once there is in existence such a system. Thus, a man has the right to be punished rather than treated if he is guilty of some offense. And, indeed, one can imagine a case in which, even in the face of an offer of a pardon, a man claims and ought to have acknowledged his right to be punished.

2. The primary reason for preferring the system of punishment as against the system of therapy might have been expressed in terms of the one system treating one as a person and the other not. In invoking the right to be punished, one justifies one's claim by reference to a more fundamental right. I want now to turn attention to this fundamental right and attempt to shed light—it will have to be little, for the topic is immense—on what is meant by 'treating an individual as a person.'

When we talk of not treating a human being as a person or 'showing no respect for one as a person' what we imply by our words is a contrast between the manner in which one acceptably responds to human beings and the manner in which one acceptably responds to animals and inanimate objects. When we treat a human being merely as an animal or some inanimate object our responses to the human being are determined, not by his choices, but ours in disregard of or with indifference to his. And when we 'look upon' a person as less than a person or not a person, we consider the person as incapable of a rational choice. In cases of not treating a human being as a person we interfere with a person in such a way that what is done, even if the person is involved in the doing, is done not by the person but by the user of the person. In extreme cases there may even be an elision of a causal chain so that we might say that *X* killed *Z* even though *Y*'s hand was the hand that held the weapon, for *Y*'s hand may have been entirely in *X*'s control. The one agent is in some way treating the other as a mere link in a causal chain. There is, of course, a wide range of cases in which a person is used to accomplish the aim of another and in which the person used is less than fully free. A person may be grabbed against his will and used as a shield. A person may be drugged or hypnotized and then employed for certain ends. A person may be deceived into doing other than he intends doing. A person may be ordered to do something and threatened with harm if he does not and coerced into doing what he does not want to. There is still another range of cases in which individuals are not used, but in which decisions by others are made that affect them in circumstances where they have the capacity for choice and where they are not being treated as persons.

But it is particularly important to look at coercion, for I have claimed that a just system of punishment treats human beings as persons; and it is not immediately apparent how ordering someone to do something and threatening harm differs essentially from having rules supported by threats of harm in case of noncompliance.

There are affinities between coercion and other cases of not treating someone as a person, for it is not the coerced person's choices but the coercer's that are responsible for what is done. But unlike other indisputable cases of not treating one as a person, for example using someone as a shield, there is some choice involved in coercion. And if this is so, why does the coercer stand in any different relation to the coerced person than the criminal law stands to individuals in society?

Suppose the person who is threatened disregards the order and gets the threatened harm. Now suppose he is told, "Well, you did after all bring it upon yourself." There is clearly something strange in this. It is the person doing the threatening and not the person threatened who is responsible. But our reaction to punishment, at least in a system that resembles the one I have described, is precisely that the person violating the rules brought it upon himself. What lies behind these different reactions?

There exist situations in the law, of course, which resemble coercion situations. There are occasions when in the law a person might justifiably say "I am not being treated as a person but being used" and where he might properly react to the punishment as something "he was hardly responsible for." But it is possible to have a system in which it would be misleading to say, over a wide range of cases of punishment for noncompliance, that we are using persons. The clearest case in which it would be inappropriate to so regard punishment would be one in which there were explicit agreement in advance that punishment should follow on the voluntary doing of certain acts. Even if one does not have such conditions satisfied, and obviously such explicit agreements are not characteristic, one can see significant differences between our system of just punishment and a coercion situation.

First, unlike the case with one person coercing another 'to do his will,' the rules in our system apply to all, with the benefits and burdens equally distributed. About such a system it cannot be said that some are being subordinated to others or are being used by others or gotten to do things by others. To the extent that the rules are thought to be to the advantage of only some or to the extent there is a maldistribution of benefits and burdens, the difference between coercion and law disappears.

Second, it might be argued that at least any person inclined to act in a manner violative of the rules stands to all others as the person coerced stands to his coercer, and that he, at least, is a person disadvantaged as others are not. It is important here, I think, that he is part of a system in which it is commonly agreed that forbearance from the acts proscribed by the rules provides advantages for all. This system is the accepted setting; it is the norm. Thus, in any coercive situation, it is the coercer who deviates from the norm, with the responsibility of the person he is attempting to coerce, defeated. In a just punishment situation, it is the person deviating from the norm, indeed he might be a coercer, who is responsible, for it is the norm to restrain oneself from acts of that kind. A voluntary agent diverging in his conduct from what is expected or what the norm is, on general causal principles, is regarded as the cause of what results from his conduct.

There is, then, some plausibility in the claim that, in a system of punishment of the kind I have sketched, a person chooses the punishment that is meted out to him. If, then, we can say in such a system that the rules provide none with advantages that others do not have, and further, that what happens to a person is conditioned by that person's choice and not that of others, then we can say that it is a system responding to one as a person.

We treat a human being as a person provided: first, we permit the person to make the choices that will determine what happens to him and second, when our responses to the person are responses respecting the person's choices. When we respond to a person's illness by treating the illness it is neither a case of treating or not treating the individual as a person. When we give a person a gift we are neither treating or not treating him as a person, unless, of course, he does not wish it, chooses not to have it, but we compel him to accept it.

3. This right to be treated as a person is a fundamental human right belonging to all human beings by virtue of their being human. It is also a natural, inalienable, and absolute right. I want now to defend these claims so reminiscent of an era of philosophical thinking about rights that many consider to have been seriously confused.

If the right is one that we possess by virtue of being human beings, we are immediately confronted with an apparent dilemma. If, to treat another as a person requires that we provide him with reasons for acting and avoid force or deception, how can we justify the force and deception we exercise with respect to children and the mentally ill? If they, too, have a right to be treated as persons are we not constantly infringing their rights? One way out of this is simply to restrict the right to those who satisfy the conditions of being a person. Infants and the insane, it might be argued, do not meet these conditions, and they would not then have the right. Another approach would be to describe the right they possess as a prima facie right to be treated as a person. This right might then be outweighed by other considerations. This approach generally seems to me, as I shall later argue, inadequate.

I prefer this tack. Children possess the right to be treated as persons but they possess this right as an individual might be said in the law of property to possess a future interest. There are advantages in talking of individuals as having a right though complete enjoyment of it is postponed. Brought to our attention, if we ascribe to them the right, is the legitimacy of their complaint if they are not provided with opportunities and conditions assuring their full enjoyment of the right when they acquire the characteristics of persons. More than this, all persons are charged with the sensitive task of not denying them the right to be a person and to be treated as a person by failing to provide the conditions for their becoming individuals who are able freely and in an informed way to choose and who are prepared themselves to assume responsibility for their choices. There is an obligation imposed upon us all, unlike that we have with respect to animals, to respond to children in such a way as to maximize the chances of their becoming persons. This may well impose upon us the obligation to treat them as persons from a very early age, that is, to respect their choices and to place upon them the responsibility for the choices to be made. There is no need to say that there is a close connection between how we respond to them and what they become. It also imposes upon us all the duty to display constantly the qualities of a person, for what they become they will largely become because of what they learn from us is acceptable behavior.

In claiming that the right is a right that human beings have by virtue of being human, there are several other features of the right, that should be noted, perhaps better conveyed by labelling them 'natural.' First, it is a right we have apart from any voluntary agreement into which we have entered. Second, it is not a right that derives from some defined position or status. Third, it is equally apparent that one has the right regardless of the society or community of which one is a member. Finally, it is a right linked to certain features of a class of beings. Were we fundamentally different than we now are, we would not have it. But it is more than that, for the right is linked to a feature of human beings which, were that feature absent—the capacity to reason and to choose on the basis of reasons—, profound conceptual changes would be involved in the thought about human beings. It is a right, then, connected with a feature of men that sets men apart from other natural phenomena.

The right to be treated as a person is inalienable. To say of a right that it is inalienable draws attention not to limitations placed on what others may do with respect to the possessor of the right but rather to limitations placed on the dispositive capacities of the possessor of the right. Something is to be gained in keeping the issues of alienability and absoluteness separate.

There are a variety of locutions qualifying what possessors of rights may and may not do. For example, on this issue of alienability, it would be worthwhile to look at, among other things, what is involved in abandoning, abdicating, conveying, giving up, granting, relinquishing, surrendering, transferring, and waiving one's rights. And with respect to each of these concepts we should also have to be sensitive to the variety of uses of the term 'rights.' What it is, for example, to waive a Hohfeldian 'right' in his strict sense will differ from what it is to waive a right in his 'privilege' sense.

Let us look at only two concepts very briefly, those of transferring and waiving rights. The clearest case of transferring rights is that of transferring rights with respect to specific objects. I own a watch and owning it I have a complicated relationship, captured in this area rather well I think by Hohfeld's four basic legal relationships, to all persons in the world with respect to the watch. We crudely capture these complex relationships by talking of my 'property rights' in or with respect to the watch. If I sell the watch, thus exercising a capacity provided by the rules of property, I have transferred rights in or with respect to the watch to someone else, the buyer, and the buyer now stands, as I formerly did, to all persons in the world in a series of complex relationships with respect to the watch.

While still the owner, I may have given to another permission to use it for several days. Had there not been the permission and had the person taken the watch, we should have spoken of interfering with or violating or, possibly, infringing my property rights. Or, to take a situation in which transferring rights is inappropriate, I may say to another "go ahead and slap me— you have my permission." In these types of situations philosophers and others have spoken of 'surrendering' rights or, alternatively and, I believe, less strangely, of 'waiving one's rights.' And recently, of course, the whole topic of 'waiving one's right to remain silent' in the context of police interrogation of suspects has been a subject of extensive litigation and discussion.

I confess to feeling that matters are not entirely perspicuous with respect to what is involved in 'waiving' or 'surrendering' rights. In conveying to another permission to take a watch or slap one, one makes legally permissible what otherwise would not have been. But in saying those words that constitute permission to take one's watch one is, of course, exercising precisely one of those capacities that leads us to say he has, while others have not, property rights with respect to the watch. Has one then waived his right in Hohfeld's strict sense in which the correlative is a duty to forebear on the part of others?

We may wish to distinguish here waiving the right to have others forbear to which there is a corresponding duty on their part to forbear, from placing oneself in a position where one has no legitimate right to complain. If I say the magic words "take the watch for a couple of days" or "go ahead and slap me," have I waived my right not to have my property taken or a right not to be struck or have I, rather, in saying what I have, simply stepped into a relation in which the rights no longer apply with respect to a specified other person? These observations find support in the following considerations. The right is that which gives rise, when infringed, to a legitimate claim against another person. What this suggests is that the right is that sphere interference with which entitles us to complain or gives us a right to complain. From this it seems to follow that a right to bodily security should be more precisely described as 'a right that others not interfere without permission.' And there is the corresponding duty not to interfere unless provided permission. Thus when we talk of waiving our rights or 'giving up our rights' in such cases we are not waiving or giving up our right to property nor our right to bodily security, for we still, of course, possess the right not to have our watch taken without permission. We have rather placed ourselves in a position where we do not possess the capacity, sometimes called a right, to complain if the person takes the watch or slaps us.

There is another type of situation in which we may speak of waiving our rights. If someone without permission slaps me, there is an infringement of my right to bodily security. If I now acquiesce or go further and say "forget it" or "you are forgiven," we might say that I had waived my right to complain. But here, too, I feel uncomfortable about what is involved. For I do have the right to complain (a right without a corresponding duty) in the event I am slapped and I have that right whether I wish it or not. If I say to another after the slap, "you are forgiven" what I do is not waive the right to complain but rather make illegitimate my subsequent exercise of that right.

Now, if we turn to the right to be treated as a person, the claim that I made was that it was inalienable, and what I meant to convey by that word of respectable age is that (a) it is a right that cannot be transferred to another in the way one's right with respect to objects can be transferred and (b) that it cannot be waived in the ways in which people talk of waiving rights to property or waiving, within certain limitations, one's right to bodily security.

While the rules of the law of property are such that persons may, satisfying certain procedures, transfer rights, the right to be treated as a person logically cannot be transferred anymore than one person can transfer to another his right to life or privacy. What, indeed, would it be like for another to have our right to be treated as a person? We can understand transferring a right with respect to certain objects. The new owner stands where the old owner stood. But with a right to be treated as a person what could this mean? My having the right meant that my choices were respected. Now if I transfer it to another this will mean that he will possess the right that my choices be respected? This is nonsense. It is only each person himself that can have his choices respected. It is no more possible to transfer this right than it is to transfer one's right to life.

Nor can the right be waived. It cannot be waived because any agreement to being treated as an animal or an instrument does not provide others with the moral permission to so treat us. One can volunteer to be a shield, but then it is one's choice on a particular occasion to be a shield. If without our permission, without our choosing it, someone used us as a shield, we may, I should suppose, forgive the person for treating us as an object. But we do not thereby waive our right to be treated as a person, for that is a right that has been infringed and what we have at most done is put ourselves in a position where it is inappropriate any longer to exercise the right to complain.

This is the sort of right, then, such that the moral rules defining relationships among persons preclude anyone from morally giving others legitimate permissions or rights with respect to one by doing or saying certain things. One stands, then, with respect to one's person as the nonowner of goods stands to those goods. The nonowner cannot, given the rule-defined relationships, convey to others rights and privileges that only the owner possesses. Just as there are agreements nonenforceable because void is contrary to public policy, so there are permissions our moral outlook regards as without moral force. With respect to being treated as a person, one is 'disabled' from modifying relations of others to one.

The right is absolute. This claim is bound to raise eyebrows. I have an innocuous point in mind in making this claim.

In discussing alienability we focused on incapacities with respect to disposing of rights. Here what I want to bring out is a sense in which a right exists despite considerations for refusing to accord the person his rights. As with the topic of alienability there are a host of concepts that deserve a close look in this area. Among them are according, acknowledging, annulling, asserting, claiming, denying, destroying, exercising, infringing, insisting upon, interfering with, possessing, recognizing and violating.

The claim that rights are absolute has been construed to

mean that 'assertions of rights cannot, for any reason under any circumstances be denied.' When there are considerations which warrant refusing to accord persons their rights, there are two prevalent views as to how this should be described: there is, first, the view that the person does not have the right, and second, the view that he has rights but of a prima facie kind and that these have been outweighed or overcome by the other considerations. "We can conceive times when such rights must give way, and, therefore, they are only prima facie and not absolute rights." (Brandt)

Perhaps there are cases in which a person claims a right to do a certain thing, say with his property, and argues that his property rights are absolute, meaning by this he has a right to do whatever he wishes with his property. Here, no doubt, it has to be explained to the person that the right he claims he has, he does not in fact possess. In such a case the person does not have and never did have, given a certain description of the right, a right that was prima facie or otherwise, to do what he claimed he had the right to do. If the assertion that a right is absolute implies that we have a right to do whatever we wish to do, it is an absurd claim and as such should not really ever have been attributed to political theorists arguing for absolute rights. But, of course, the claim that we have a prima facie right to do whatever we wish to do is equally absurd. The right is not prima facie either, for who would claim, thinking of the right to be free, that one has a prima facie right to kill others, if one wishes, unless there are moral considerations weighing against it?

There are, however, other situations in which it is accepted by all that a person possesses rights of a certain kind, and the difficulty we face is that of according the person the right he is claiming when this will promote more evil than good. The just act is to give the man his due and giving a man what it is his right to have is giving him his due. But it is a mistake to suppose that justice is the only dimension of morality. It may be justifiable not to accord to a man his rights. But it is no less a wrong to him, no less an infringement. It is seriously misleading to turn all justifiable infringements into noninfringements by saying that the right is only prima facie, as if we have, in concluding that we should not accord a man his rights, made out a case that he had none. To use the language of 'prima facie rights' misleads, for it suggests that a presumption of the existence of a right has been overcome in these cases where all that can be said is that the presumption in favor of according a man his rights has been overcome. If we begin to think the right itself is prima facie, we shall, in cases in which we are justified in not according it, fail sufficiently to bring out that we have interfered where justice says we should not. Our moral framework is unnecessarily and undesirably impoverished by the theory that there are such rights.

When I claim, then, that the right to be treated as a person is absolute what I claim is that given that one is a person, one always has the right so to be treated, and that while there may possibly be occasions morally requiring not according a person this right, this fact makes it no less true that the right exists and would be infringed if the person were not accorded it.

4. Having said something about the nature of this fundamental right I want now, in conclusion, to suggest that the denial of this right entails the denial of all moral rights and duties. This requires bringing out what is surely intuitively clear that any framework of rights and duties presupposes individuals that have the capacity to choose on the basis of reasons presented to them, and that what makes legitimate actions within such a system are the free choices of individuals. There is, in other words, a distribution of benefits and burdens in accord with a respect for the freedom of choice and freedom of action of all. I think that the best way to make this point may be to sketch some of the features of a world in which rights and duties are possessed.

First, rights exist only when there is some conception of some things valued and others not. Secondly, and implied in the first point, is the fact that there are dispositions to defend the valued commodities. Third, the valued commodities may be interfered with by others in this world. A group of animals might be said to satisfy these first three conditions. Fourth, rights exist when there are recognized rules establishing the legitimacy of some acts and ruling out others. Mistakes in the claim of right are possible. Rights imply the concepts of interference and infringement, concepts the elucidation of which requires the concept of a rule applying to the conduct of persons. Fifth, to possess a right is to possess something that constitutes a legitimate restraint on the freedom of action of others. It is clear, for example, that if individuals were incapable of controlling their actions we would have no notion of a legitimate claim that they do so. If, for example, we were all disposed to object or disposed to complain, as the elephant seal is disposed to object when his territory is invaded, then the objection would operate in a causal way, or approximating a causal way, in getting the behavior of noninterference. In a system of rights, on the other hand, there is a point to appealing to the rules in legitimating one's complaint. Implied, then, in any conception of rights are the existence of individuals capable of choosing and capable of choosing on the basis of considerations with respect to rules. The distribution of freedom throughout such a system is determined by the free choice of individuals. Thus any denial of the right to be treated as a person would be a denial undercutting the whole system, for the system rests on the assumption that spheres of legitimate and illegitimate conduct are to be delimited with regard to the choices made by persons.

This conclusion stimulates one final reflection on the therapy world we imagined.

The denial of this fundamental right will also carry with it, ironically, the denial of the right to treatment to those who are ill. In the world as we now understand it, there are those who do wrong and who have a right to be responded to as persons who have done wrong. And there are those who have not done wrong but who are suffering from illnesses that in a variety of ways interfere with their capacity to live their lives as complete persons. These persons who are ill have a claim upon our compassion. But more than this they have, as animals do not, a right to be treated as persons. When an individual is ill he is entitled to that assistance which will make it possible for him to resume his functioning as a person. If it is an injustice to punish an innocent person, it is no less an injustice, and a far more significant one in our day, to fail to promote as best we can through adequate facilities and medical care the treatment of those who are ill. Those human beings who fill our mental institutions are entitled to more than they do in fact receive; they should be viewed as possessing the right to be treated as a person so that our responses to them may increase the likelihood that they will enjoy fully the right to be so treated. Like the child the mentally ill person has a future interest we cannot rightly deny him. Society is today sensitive to the infringement of justice in punishing the innocent; elaborate rules exist to avoid this evil. Society should be no less sensitive to the injustice of failing to bring back to the community of persons those whom it is possible to bring back.

Appendix I

The Virginia Declaration of Rights, June 12, 1776

A declaration of rights, made by the Representatives of the good People of Virginia, assembled in full and free Convention, which rights do pertain to them and their posterity as the basis and foundation of government.

I. That all men are by nature equally free and independent, and have certain inherent rights, of which, when they enter into a state of society, they cannot by any compact deprive or divest their posterity; namely, the enjoyment of life and liberty, with the means of acquiring and possessing property, and pursuing and obtaining happiness and safety.

II. That all power is vested in, and consequently derived from, the people; that magistrates are their trustees and servants, and at all times amenable to them.

III. That government is, or ought to be, instituted for the common benefit, protection, and security of the people, nation or community; of all the various modes and forms of government, that is best which is capable of producing the greatest degree of happiness and safety, and is most effectually secured against the danger of maladministration; and that, when a government shall be found inadequate or contrary to these purposes, a majority of the community hath an indubitable, unalienable, and indefeasible right to reform, alter or abolish it, in such manner as shall be judged most conducive to the public weal.

IV. That no man, or set of men, are entitled to exclusive or separate emoluments or privileges from the community but in consideration of public services, which not being descendible, neither ought the offices of magistrate, legislator or judge to be hereditary.

V. That the legislative, executive and judicial powers should be separate and distinct; and that the members thereof may be restrained from oppression, by feeling and participating the burthens of the people, they should, at fixed periods, be re-

duced to a private station, return into that body from which
they were originally taken, and the vacancies be supplied by
frequent, certain and regular elections, in which all, or any part
of the former members to be again eligible or ineligible, as the
laws shall direct.

VI. That all elections ought to be free, and that all men
having sufficient evidence of permanent common interest with,
and attachment to the community, have the right of suffrage,
and cannot be taxed, or deprived of their property for public
uses, without their own consent, or that of their representatives
so elected, nor bound by any law to which they have not in like
manner assented, for the public good.

VII. That all power of suspending laws, or the execution of
laws, by any authority, without consent of the representatives
of the people, is injurious to their rights, and ought not to be
exercised.

VIII. That in all capital or criminal prosecutions a man hath a
right to demand the cause and nature of his accusation, to be
confronted with the accusers and witnesses, to call for evidence in his favour, and to a speedy trial by an impartial jury of
twelve men of his vicinage, without whose unanimous consent
he cannot be found guilty; nor can he be compelled to give
evidence against himself; that no man be deprived of his
liberty, except by the law of the land or the judgment of his
peers.

IX. That excessive bail ought not to be required, nor excessive fines imposed, nor cruel and unusual punishments inflicted.

X. That general warrants, whereby an officer or messenger
may be commanded to search suspected places without evidence of a fact committed, or to seize any person or persons
not named, or whose offence is not particularly described and
supported by evidence, are grievous and oppressive, and
ought not to be granted.

XI. That in controversies respecting property, and in suits
between man and man, the ancient trial by jury of twelve men
is preferable to any other, and ought to be held sacred.

XII. That the freedom of the press is one of the great bul-
warks of liberty, and can never be restrained but by despotic
governments.

XIII. That a well-regulated militia, composed of the body of
the people, trained to arms, is the proper, natural and safe
defence of a free State; that standing armies in time of peace
should be avoided as dangerous to liberty; and that in all cases

the military should be under strict subordination to, and governed by, the civil power.

XIV. That the people have a right to uniform government; and therefore that no government separate from or independent of the government of Virginia ought to be erected or established within the limits thereof.

XV. That no free government, or the blessing of liberty, can be preserved to any people, but by a firm adherence to justice, moderation, temperance, frugality and virtue, and by a frequent recurrence to fundamental principles.

XVI. That religion, or the duty which we owe to our Creator, and the manner of discharging it, can be directed only by reason and conviction, not by force or violence; and therefore all men are equally entitled to the free exercise of religion, according to the dictates of conscience; and that it is the duty of all to practice Christian forbearance, love and charity towards each other.

Appendix II

Extract from the Declaration of Independence of the United States of America, July 4, 1776

**The Unanimous Declaration
of the Thirteen United States
of America**

138   When in the Course of human events, it becomes necessary for
one people to dissolve the political bands which have connected them with another, and to assume among the Powers of
the earth, the separate and equal station to which the Laws of
Nature and of Nature's God entitle them, a decent respect to
the opinions of mankind requires that they should declare the
causes which impel them to the separation.

We hold these truths to be self-evident, that all men are
created equal, that they are endowed by their Creator with
certain unalienable Rights, that among these are Life, Liberty
and the pursuit of Happiness. That to secure these rights,
Governments are instituted among Men, deriving their just
powers from the consent of the governed, That whenever any
Form of Government becomes destructive of these ends, it is
the Right of the People to alter or to abolish it, and to institute
new Government, laying its foundation on such principles and
organizing its powers in such form, as to them shall seem most
likely to effect their Safety and Happiness. Prudence, indeed,
will dictate that Governments long established should not be
changed for light and transient causes; and accordingly all
experience hath shown, that mankind are more disposed to
suffer, while evils are sufferable, than to right themselves by
abolishing the forms to which they are accustomed. But when a
long train of abuses and usurpations, pursuing invariably the
same Object, evinces a design to reduce them under absolute

Despotism, it is their right, it is their duty, to throw off such Government, and to provide new Guards for their future security.—Such has been the patient sufferance of these Colonies; and such is now the necessity which constrains them to alter their former Systems of Government. The history of the present King of Great Britain is a history of repeated injuries and usurpations, all having in direct object the establishment of an absolute Tyranny over these States. To prove this, let facts be submitted to a candid world.

[Then follow statements of particular grievances.]

In every stage of these Oppressions We have Petitioned for Redress in the most humble terms: Our repeated Petitions have been answered only by repeated injury. A Prince, whose character is thus marked by every act which may define a Tyrant, is unfit to be the ruler of a free People.

Nor have We been wanting in attention to our British brethren. We have warned them from time to time of attempts by their legislature to extend an unwarrantable jurisdiction over us. We have reminded them of the circumstances of our emigration and settlement here. We have appealed to their native justice and magnanimity, and we have conjured them by the ties of our common kindred to disavow these usurpations, which would inevitably interrupt our connections and correspondence. They too have been deaf to the voice of justice and of consanguinity. We must, therefore, acquiesce in the necessity which denounces our Separation, and hold them, as we hold the rest of mankind, Enemies in War, in Peace Friends.

We, therefore, the Representatives of the United States of America, in General Congress, Assembled, appealing to the Supreme Judge of the world for the rectitude of our intentions, do, in the Name, and by Authority of the good People of these Colonies, solemnly publish and declare, That these United Colonies are, and of Right ought to be Free and Independent States; that they are Absolved from all Allegiance to the British Crown, and that all political connection between them and the State of Great Britain, is and ought to be totally dissolved; and that as Free and Independent States, they have full Power to levy War, conclude Peace, contract Alliances, establish Commerce, and to do all other Acts and Things which Independent States may of right do. And for the support of this Declaration, with a firm reliance on the Protection of Divine Providence, we mutually pledge to each other our Lives, our Fortunes and our sacred Honor.

Appendix III

Declaration of the Rights of Man and of Citizens (1789)

140 The representatives of the people of France, formed into a National Assembly, considering that ignorance, neglect, or contempt of human rights, are the sole causes of public misfortunes and corruptions of Government, have resolved to set forth in a solemn declaration, these natural, imprescriptible, and inalienable rights: that this declaration being constantly present to the minds of the members of the body social, they may be for ever kept attentive to their rights and their duties; that the acts of the legislative and executive powers of government, being capable of being every moment compared with the end of political institutions, may be more respected; and also, that the future claims of the citizens, being directed by simple and incontestible principles, may always tend to the maintenance of the Constitution, and the general happiness.

For these reasons, the National Assembly doth recognise and declare, in the presence of the Supreme Being, and with the hope of his blessing and favour, the following *sacred* rights of men and of citizens:

I. Men are born, and always continue, free and equal in respect of their rights. Civil distinctions, therefore, can be founded only on public utility.

II. The end of all political associations, is the preservation of the natural and imprescriptible rights of man; and these rights are liberty, property, security, and resistance of oppression.

III. The nation is essentially the source of all sovereignty; nor can any individual, or any body of men, be entitled to any authority which is not expressly derived from it.

IV. Political liberty consists in the power of doing whatever does not injure another. The exercise of the natural rights of every man, has no other limits than those which are necessary

Prefixed to the French Constitution of 1791. The translation is by Thomas Paine as it appears in his *Rights of Man*.

to secure to every *other* man the free exercise of the same rights; and these limits are determinable only by the law.

V. The law ought to prohibit only actions hurtful to society. What is not prohibited by the law, should not be hindered; nor should any one be compelled to that which the law does not require.

VI. The law is an expression of the will of the community. All citizens have a right to concur, either personally, or by their representatives, in its formation. It should be the same to all, whether it protects or punishes; and all being equal in its sight, are equally eligible to all honours, places, and employments, according to their different abilities, without any other distinction than that created by their virtues and talents.

VII. No man should be accused, arrested, or held in confinement, except in cases determined by the law, and according to the forms which it has prescribed. All who promote, solicit, execute, or cause to be executed, arbitrary orders, ought to be punished, and every citizen called upon, or apprehended by virtue of the law, ought immediately to obey, and renders himself culpable by resistance.

VIII. The law ought to impose no other penalties but such as are absolutely and evidently necessary; and no one ought to be punished, but in virtue of a law promulgated before the offence, and legally applied.

IX. Every man being presumed innocent till he has been convicted, whenever his detention becomes indispensable, all rigour to him, more than is necessary to secure his person, ought to be provided against by the law.

X. No man ought to be molested on account of his opinions, not even on account of his *religious* opinions, provided his avowal of them does not disturb the public order established by the law.

XI. The unrestrained communication of thoughts and opinions being one of the most precious rights of man, every citizen may speak, write, and publish freely, provided he is responsible for the abuse of this liberty, in cases determined by the law.

XII. A public force being necessary to give security to the rights of men and of citizens, that force is instituted for the benefit of the community and not for the particular benefit of the persons to whom it is intrusted.

XIII. A common contribution being necessary for the support of the public force, and for defraying the other expenses of government, it ought to be divided equally among the members of the community, according to their abilities.

XIV. Every citizen has a right, either by himself or his representative, to a free voice in determining the necessity of public contributions, the appropriation of them, and their amount, mode of assessment, and duration.

XV. Every community has had a right to demand of all its agents an account of their conduct.

XVI. Every community in which a separation of powers and a security of rights is not provided for, wants a constitution.

XVII. The right to property being inviolable and sacred, no one ought to be deprived of it, except in cases of evident public necessity, legally ascertained, and on condition of a previous just indemnity.

Appendix IV

Universal Declaration
of Human Rights

Whereas Member States have pledged themselves to achieve, **143**
in co-operation with the United Nations, the promotion of universal respect for and observance of human rights and fundamental freedoms,

Whereas a common understanding of these rights and freedoms is of the greatest importance for the full realisation of
this pledge,

Now, therefore, the General Assembly, Proclaim this Universal
Declaration of Human Rights as a common standard of
achievement for all peoples and all nations, to the end that
every individual and every organ of society, keeping this Declaration constantly in mind, shall strive by teaching and education to promote respect for these rights and freedoms and by
progressive measures, national and international, to secure
their universal and effective recognition and observance, both
among the peoples of Member States themselves and among
the peoples of territories under their jurisdiction.

Article 1

All human beings are born free and equal in dignity and rights.
They are endowed with reason and conscience and should act
towards one another in a spirit of brotherhood.

Article 2

1. Everyone is entitled to all the rights and freedoms set forth
in this Declaration, without distinction of any kind, such as
race, colour, sex, language, religion, political or other opinion,
national or social origin, property, birth or other status.

Adopted on December 10th, 1948 by General Assembly of United Nations
at the Palais de Chaillot, Paris.

2. Furthermore, no distinction shall be made on the basis of the political, jurisdictional or international status of the country or territory to which a person belongs, whether it be independent, trust, non-self-governing or under any other limitation of sovereignty.

Article 3

Everyone has the right to life, liberty and security of person.

Article 4

No one shall be held in slavery or servitude; slavery and the slave trade shall be prohibited in all their forms.

Article 5

No one shall be subjected to torture or to cruel, inhuman or degrading treatment or punishment.

Article 6

Everyone has the right to recognition everywhere as a person before the law.

Article 7

All are equal before the law and are entitled without any discrimination to equal protection of the law. All are entitled to equal protection against any discrimination in violation of this Declaration and against any incitement to such discrimination.

Article 8

Everyone has the right to an effective remedy by the competent national tribunals for acts violating the fundamental rights granted him by the constitution or by law.

Article 9

No one shall be subjected to arbitrary arrest, detention or exile.

Article 10

Everyone is entitled in full equality to a fair and public hearing by an independent and impartial tribunal, in the determination of his rights and obligations and of any criminal charge against him.

Article 11

1. Everyone charged with a penal offence has the right to be presumed innocent until proved guilty according to law in a public trial at which he has had all the guarantees necessary for his defence.
2. No one shall be held guilty of any penal offence on account of any act or omission which did not constitute a penal offence, under national or international law, at the time when it was committed. Nor shall a heavier penalty be imposed than the one that was applicable at the time the penal offence was committed.

Article 12

No one shall be subjected to arbitrary interference with his privacy, family, home or correspondence, nor to attacks upon his honour and reputation. Everyone has the right to the protection of the law against such interference or attacks.

Article 13

1. Everyone has the right to freedom of movement and residence within the borders of each State.
2. Everyone has the right to leave any country, including his own, and to return to his country.

Article 14

1. Everyone has the right to seek and to enjoy in other countries asylum from persecution.
2. This right may not be invoked in the case of prosecutions genuinely arising from non-political crimes or from acts contrary to the purposes and principles of the United Nations.

Article 15

1. Everyone has the right to a nationality.
2. No one shall be arbitrarily deprived of his nationality nor denied the right to change his nationality.

Article 16

1. Men and women of full age, without any limitation due to race, nationality or religion, have the right to marry and to found a family. They are entitled to equal rights as to marriage, during marriage and at its dissolution.
2. Marriage shall be entered into only with the free and full consent of the intending spouses.
3. The family is the natural and fundamental group unit of society and is entitled to protection by society and the State.

Article 17

1. Everyone has the right to own property alone as well as in association with others.
2. No one shall be arbitrarily deprived of his property.

Article 18

Everyone has the right to freedom of thought, conscience and religion; this right includes freedom to change his religion or belief, and freedom, either alone or in community with others and in public or private, to manifest his religion or belief in teaching, practice, worship and observance.

Article 19

Everyone has the right to freedom of opinion and expression; this right includes freedom to hold opinions without interference and to seek, receive and impart information and ideas through any media and regardless of frontiers.

Article 20

1. Everyone has the right to freedom of peaceful assembly and association.
2. No one may be compelled to belong to an association.

1. Everyone has the right to take part in the government of his country, directly or through freely chosen representatives.
2. Everyone has the right of equal access to public service in his country.
3. The will of the people shall be the basis of the authority of government; this will shall be expressed in periodic and genuine elections which shall be by universal and equal suffrage and shall be held by secret vote or by equivalent free voting procedures.

Everyone, as a member of society, has the right to social security and is entitled to realisation, through national effort and international co-operation and in accordance with the organisation and resources of each State, of the economic, social and cultural rights indispensable for his dignity and the free development of his personality.

1. Everyone has the right to work, to free choice of employment, to just and favourable conditions of work and to protection against unemployment.
2. Everyone, without any discrimination, has the right to equal pay for equal work.
3. Everyone who works has the right to just and favourable remuneration ensuring for himself and his family an existence worthy of human dignity, and supplemented, if necessary, by other means of social protection.
4. Everyone has the right to form and to join trade unions for the protection of his interests.

Everyone has the right to rest and leisure, including reasonable limitation of working hours and periodic holidays with pay.

1. Everyone has the right to a standard of living adequate for the health and well-being of himself and of his family, including

food, clothing, housing and medical care and necessary social services, and the right to security in the event of unemployment, sickness, disability, widowhood, old age or other lack of livelihood in circumstances beyond his control.

2. Motherhood and childhood are entitled to special care and assistance. All children, whether born in or out of wedlock, shall enjoy the same social protection.

Article 26

1. Everyone has the right to education. Education shall be free, at least in the elementary and fundamental stages. Elementary education shall be compulsory. Technical and professional education shall be made generally available and higher education shall be equally accessible to all on the basis of merit.

2. Education shall be directed to the full development of the human personality and to the strengthening of respect for human rights and fundamental freedoms. It shall promote understanding, tolerance and friendship among all nations, racial or religious groups, and shall further the activities of the United Nations for the maintenance of peace.

3. Parents have a prior right to choose the kind of education that shall be given to their children.

Article 27

1. Everyone has the right freely to participate in the cultural life of the community, to enjoy the arts and to share in scientific advancement and its benefits.

2. Everyone has the right to the protection of the moral and material interests resulting from any scientific, literary or artistic production of which he is the author.

Article 28

Everyone is entitled to a social and international order in which the rights and freedoms set forth in this Declaration can be fully realised.

Article 29

1. Everyone has duties to the community in which alone the free and full development of his personality is possible.

2. In the exercise of his rights and freedoms, everyone shall be subject only to such limitations as are determined by law solely

for the purpose of securing due recognition and respect for the rights and freedoms of others and of meeting the just requirements of morality, public order and the general welfare in a democratic society.

3. These rights and freedoms may in no case be exercised contrary to the purposes and principles of the United Nations.

Article 30

Nothing in this Declaration may be interpreted as implying for any State, group or person any right to engage in any activity or to perform any act aimed at the destruction of any of the rights and freedoms set forth herein.

Bibliography

150 The following will be helpful to the student who wishes to pursue further study of the topics dealt with in the essays included in this volume.

A. Natural Law and Natural or Human Rights

Aquinas, St. Thomas. *Treatise on Law,* in *Summa Theologica* (Anton C. Pegis, ed.). New York: Random House, 1945. Vol. 2, pp. 742–978.

Bedau, Hugo. *The Right to Life and Other Essays on the Death Penalty.* New York: Pegasus, 1969.

Bosanquet, Bernard. *Philosophical Theory of the State.* 4th ed. New York: St. Martin's Press, 1923.

Brinton, Crane. "Natural Rights," in *The Encyclopedia of Social Science.* New York: Macmillan Co., 1933. Vol. 11.

Brown, Stuart M., Jr. "Inalienable Rights," *Philosophical Review,* Vol. 64, No. 2 (1955).

Cicero. *De Re Publica,* Book 3, and *De Legibus,* Book 1 (C. W. Keyes, trans. and ed.). London: Loeb Classical Library, 1928.

Cranston, Maurice William. *What Are Human Rights?* New York: Basic Books, 1963.

Entreves, A. P. d'. *Natural Law.* London: Hutchinson's University Library, 1951.

Feinberg, Joel. "Wasserstrom on Human Rights," *Journal of Philosophy* (October 29, 1964).

Frankena, W. K. "The Concept of Universal Human Rights," in *Science, Language and Human Rights*. Philadelphia: University of Pennsylvania Press, 1952. Pp. 189–207.

————. "Natural and Inalienable Rights," *Philosophical Review,* Vol. 64, No. 2 (1955).

Gierke, O. F. *Natural Law and the Theory of Society* (E. Barker, trans.). Cambridge, Eng.: Cambridge University Press, 1934. Reprinted Boston: Beacon Press, 1957.

Green, T. H. *Lectures on the Principles of Political Obligation.* New York: Humanities Press, 1966.

Hobbes, Thomas. *Leviathan,* 1651. Edited with an introduction by W. G. Pogson Smith. Oxford: Clarendon Press, 1958.

Human Rights: Comments and Interpretations. A symposium edited by UNESCO. New York: Columbia University Press, 1949.

Macpherson, C. B. *The Political Theory of Possessive Individualism: Hobbes to Locke.* Oxford: Clarendon Press, 1962.

Maritain, Jacques. *The Rights of Man and Natural Law.* New York: Charles Scribner's, 1943.

Melden, A. I. "The Concept of Universal Human Rights," in *Science, Language and Human Rights*. Philadelphia: University of Pennsylvania Press, 1952. Pp. 167–188.

Moskowitz, M. *Human Rights and World Order.* New York: Oceana Publications, 1958.

Owens, Meirlys. "The Notion of Human Rights: A Reconsideration," *American Philosophical Quarterly,* Vol. 6, No. 3 (July 1969).

Paine, T. *The Rights of Man,* 1791. New York: E. P. Dutton (Everyman's Library), 1951.

Raphael, D. D. (ed.). *Political Theory and the Rights of Man.* Bloomington: Indiana University Press, 1967.

Ritchie, D. G. *Natural Rights.* London: G. Allen and Unwin, 1952.

Spinoza, Benedict. *Tractatus Theologica-Politicus,* 1670, and *Tractatus Politicus,* 1677. A. G. Wernham, trans. and ed., in *Benedict de Spinoza: The Political Works.* Oxford: Clarendon Press, 1958.

Strauss, Leo. *Natural Right and History.* Chicago: University of Chicago Press, 1963.

B. Moral Rights

Bedau, H. "Rights as Claims, Reasons and Needs," *Akten des XIV Internationalen Kongresses für Philosophie,* 1968.

Benn, S. I. "Rights" in *Encyclopedia of Philosophy* (P. Edwards, ed.). New York: Macmillan Co., 1967. Vol. 7, pp. 195–199.

Braybrooke, David. Part 1 ("Personal Rights") in *Three Tests for Democracy.* New York: Random House, 1968.

Carritt, E. F. *Ethical and Political Thinking.* Oxford: Clarendon Press, 1947.

Ewing, A. C. Chapter 2 of *The Individual, the State and World Government.* New York: Macmillan Co., 1947.

Feinberg, Joel. "Duties, Rights and Claims," *American Philosophical Quarterly,* Vol. 3, No. 2 (April 1966).

Hart, H. L. A. "The Ascription of Responsibility and Rights," in *Logic and Language* (A. Flew, ed.). Oxford: Basil Blackwell, 1951.

Lyons, David. "Rights, Claimants, and Beneficiaries," *American Philosophical Quarterly,* Vol. 6, No. 3 (July 1969).

Mabbott, J. B. *The State and the Citizen.* London: Arrow, 1958.

McCloskey, H. J. "Rights," *The Philosophical Quarterly,* Vol. 15 (1965).

Melden, A. I. *Rights and Right Conduct.* Oxford: Basil Blackwell, 1959.

Ross, W. D. *The Right and the Good.* Oxford: Basil Blackwell, 1961. Pp. 48–56.

C. Legal Rights

Austin, John. *The Province of Jurisprudence Determined,* 1832. Edited with an introduction by H. L. A. Hart. London: Weidenfeld and Nicolson, 1954.

Hägerström, Axel. *Enquiries into the Nature of Law and Morals.* C. D. Broad, trans.; Karl Olivecrona, ed. Stockholm: Almquist and Wiksell, 1953.

Hohfeld, Wesley H. *Fundamental Legal Conceptions,* 1919. New Haven: Yale University Press, 1964.

Pound, Roscoe. *Jurisprudence.* St. Paul, Minnesota: West Publishing Co., 1959. Vol. 4.

Ross, Alf. *On Law and Justice.* Berkeley: University of California Press, 1959.